NOT ON
THE HIGH
STREET
.com

for a life less ordinary

As someone whose opinion we value,
we're very excited to be able to share
this, our second book, with you!

We hope that you enjoy reading our
story and the lessons we've learnt
along the way.

Holly Tozhie

SHAPE UP YOUR BUSINESS

Also by Sophie Cornish and Holly Tucker
Build a Business from Your Kitchen Table

SHAPE UP YOUR BUSINESS

THE FOUNDERS OF NOTONTHEHIGHSTREET.COM
SHARE THEIR STORY IN A *30-day success plan*

*Sophie Cornish and Holly Tucker
with Jessica Fellowes*

**SIMON &
SCHUSTER**

London · New York · Sydney · Toronto · New Delhi

A CBS COMPANY

First published in Great Britain by Simon & Schuster UK Ltd, 2014
A CBS COMPANY

1 3 5 7 9 10 8 6 4 2

Simon & Schuster UK Ltd
1st Floor
222 Gray's Inn Road
London WC1X 8HB

www.simonandschuster.co.uk

Simon & Schuster Australia, Sydney
Simon & Schuster India, New Delhi

A CIP catalogue record for this book is available
from the British Library

Flexibound ISBN: 978-1-47110-214-1
eBook ISBN: 978-1-47110-216-5

The author and publishers have made all reasonable efforts to
contact copyright-holders for permission, and apologise for any omissions
or errors in the form of credits given. Corrections may be made to future printings.

Designed by Lydia Ripper
Back cover photo by Dan Duchars
Photographed paper artwork by Neil Mersh
Typeset in the UK by M Rules

Printed in Italy by L.E.G.O SpA

For Ollie, Honor
and Harry

Contents

Letter to the reader

'I said, "Somebody should do something about that."
Then I realized I am somebody.'

LILY TOMLIN

Dear reader

Thank you for picking up our book. We're here to give you the inside scoop on what it's *really* like to run and grow a business. We've been doing it ourselves for several years, as well as helping thousands of small businesses attain success, and now we want the same for you, too. It's not going to be easy – we've had to face up to hard truths about ourselves and notonthehighstreet.com in order to make ourselves better and we're going to ask the same of you. But the end result is worth it – knowing who you are and how best you can run your business will enable you to reach heights you had hardly dared to dream of.

This book is proudly for entrepreneurs: those who are self-starters when it comes to making their business ideas happen. Those who have the ability to make something from nothing – you don't need a job description, just a vision that you're working towards. Like being in love, you don't care how much it wants of you; in fact you want it to take up all of your time because it's where you belong. There's a fluttery, excited feeling about the promise of success and everything that means to you. But perhaps you don't know quite how you're going to get there yet. That's what we're here for.

Not all entrepreneurs are running their own businesses – it's a mindset as much as anything. Entrepreneurs may work for someone else, but it's their attitude to themselves and the business they're in that sets them apart from the clock-watchers. So whether you work for yourself or for someone else, whether you work from home or in an office, whether you own a business or only dream of it, this book is for you. Those at the top of fast-moving and ambitious businesses share a set of skills, an attitude and a confidence that got them there and keeps them there. Sometimes these things are innate but not always – they can be learned and we're going to teach you them in this book.

Something else ... This book is principally for women. Of course men can learn from the lessons within – and we'd like them to! – but we don't want to shy away from the facts: firstly, that the majority of our customers and our small-business partners are currently women, so we understand what makes them tick, what motivates them and what their issues are; and secondly, that there seems to be a new wave of feminism being discussed, one that acknowledges that both men and women are, in the main, onside but that we need to bring about some deep cultural changes in order for our shared desire of true gender equality – at work and at home – to be made real.

Part of this book is a call-to-arms for women in business, but it's mainly about guiding women through the steps they must necessarily take in order to take charge of their business life and improve it.

Because at notonthehighstreet.com we believe in a life less ordinary. For our customers, of course, this means offering them the chance to discover and own beautiful, out-of-the-ordinary things when it matters to them. For our sellers, it means giving them the chance to determine their own future by doing something they love and working on their own terms, perhaps for the first time in their lives. For our team, it means they work in a business that they really enjoy and believe in, every day. We want a life less ordinary for you, our readers, too.

We'll help you identify your goals – both short and long term – and work out how to achieve them. We'll show you how you can learn confidence, which will in turn improve your negotiation skills. The daily grind may have started to wear you down but we can show you how to fall in love with your business all over again. You'll learn that the most important product you're selling is yourself and that at work everyone is a customer.

Too many women are afraid of money – the language around it as much as putting a price on their worth – we'll give you the courage (and lingo) you need. We'll give you the tools you need to talk to the team you work with clearly and honestly. Finally, we'll give the raw truth about how going for your business goals impacts on your personal life and relationships – it's not always pretty but it can be good too. We'll be open about our own mistakes and the lessons we learned from them and we'll hear from some of the partners – the makers, designers and sellers that trade through notonthehighstreet.com.

In the final analysis, *you* are your business and your career and that's why you need to look at the emotive as well as the pragmatic aspects of the way in which you earn your wage, whether you pay yourself or someone else does. All we require is a thirty-day commitment to turn around the next thirty years. Make these changes and you'll control your own destiny. Don't – and someone else will.

To those of you that read our first book, *Build a Business from Your Kitchen Table* – for which, thank you – we may have given the impression that after the trials and tribulations of the first two years, during which we launched notonthehighstreet.com, had a storming first year, nearly went broke, recovered and hit our first million-pound turnover, we more or less rode off into the sunset. Well, this is where the needle scratches across the record and starts to play again because it wasn't quite like that. The truth is, it isn't like that for *anyone.*

This book is here to talk about the crucial stage in any company – the bit just after you've survived the first year or two, when complacency (or at least a heavy weariness) sets in and then ... the wake-up call happens. Because believe us, if you think your business is running itself then soon it's going to start running you. It can only mean you've taken your eye off the ball and something is going to need fixing very soon.

Many find that the daily grind of keeping a business going takes the love out of it and they can no longer remember what got them excited in the first place. Other businesses fail because the owners or key employees keep putting off dealing with the aspects they find uncomfortable – whether that's finance, PR, HR or marketing – and then discover too late that the one rotten apple has soured the whole barrel.

We know these things because we've come dangerously close to all of them ourselves and, of course, we've seen them happen to our partners. We wanted to write this book to help businesswomen find their zest for their life's work. If it's been feeling sluggish then we can help get it moving – perhaps you need to remember why you wanted to start your business in the first place or maybe you need to make sure you're managing it correctly. We'll show you how to take apart your business, check it, analyse it correctly and put it back together again. And because *you* are your business, and the mood you're in affects the way it works, as well as those who may be working for and with you, we want to help you look at your own health, your relationships and your support structure to make sure that you are always operating at the very best you can be.

Why thirty days? We believe that it's a reasonable time span for a commitment to change. Many of the country's top business coaches – and we've been talking to some of them for this book – ask their clients to commit to 'thirty-day challenges'. It's believed that significant change in this period is obtainable because it is not so long that it becomes too hard to keep up but nor is it so short that there's no chance of effectiveness. Whatever your goal is, you will need to assess each area of your business to be certain that you are fixing the right thing. And it may be that a weakness in one area is affecting another that doesn't immediately appear to be related. To achieve this level of change, you may have to pull in favours and this you can do for a month, but no longer. You don't, of course, have to do all the thirty days non-stop. But you do have to make room for them in your life – the sooner, the better.

Each chapter looks at a different area in your life, skills and business that needs to be explored, analysed, tested, learned and worked on in order to achieve success. There are practical exercises in each chapter, some of which are quick – less than an hour – some of which will require hard work and thought. If you are not able to devote a single time slot to an exercise, that's fine – break it down into time frames you can afford across a few days but make sure you complete them in the order in which they are set out.

Any resources that we either mention or simply think would be helpful are listed in The Directory. And while we try to keep obtuse business words to a minimum, some phrases are part of the language. If there's anything you don't understand, you should be able to find it in the Jargon Buster.

One other thing. This isn't a one-off fix-it. This book should be referred to throughout the lifespan of your business, so use it like an annual MOT.

There are no rights and wrongs but you may find that you have been doing things in such a way that they are not beneficial to you or your business. That's fine: you'll learn from those errors and that makes them valuable.

If we did it, you can. Good luck.

Sophie Cornish and Holly Tucker
Founders, notonthehighstreet.com

Meet the Partners

Throughout the book, we asked some of our partners to give us their insight and stories on the different areas of their business and home lives. Here's a little background on each of them. We are proud to work with 5,000 partners, representing a wide range from the single designer-maker working off the kitchen table to the large studios turning over hundreds of thousands of pounds a year.

Bookishly

Louise Verity created Bookishly in 2009, having started a collection of rescued books, comics and sheet music, and uses her typography skills to repurpose them into works of art. The business is very much in the family – Louise uses the family framing business to finish her designs. Personal, creative and charming, Bookishly has tapped into the nostalgic hole left by e-readers in the modern age.

My 1st Years

Specialising in personalised newborn gifts and accessories, My 1st Years has expanded quickly since starting in 2010, using innovative product design and creating an exceptionally easy way for customers to order exceptional products. Founders Daniel Price and Jonny Sitton have created a brand through their passion and vision to deliver a great customer experience.

Becky Broome

Originally a textile designer, Becky vastly expanded her product range and business capacity in 2013 to encompass personalised glassware and homeware. Her husband Kristian joined the business full time and they collaborated with Becky's father to use his factory and warehouse space, making this a true family business.

Oakdene Designs

Oakdene Designs is made up of a small team of budding designers and manufacturers in a small village near Dorking, Surrey. Every single product is specially made to order in their studios and materials are sourced throughout the UK.

Highland Angel

Created by Yvonne Carmichael, Highland Angel focuses on making classic jewellery personal and extraordinary. Her two daughters joined the business following early success and between them they produce an ever-growing range from their studio in Edinburgh.

Ellie Ellie

A powerhouse of entrepreneurial spirit, Ellie Ellie founder Danielle Plowman has built a business based on redesigned, recycled and re-loved gifts, many of which are personalised and made to order. Embracing the best of British, her products have a nostalgic and playful feel.

Maria Allen

Brighton-based designer Maria Allen has created a sought-after collection of illustrated and personalised jewellery using her illustrations and keen eye for trends and innovative design. Themes such as travel, typography and romance feature throughout her designs, which have all been developed with creative customers in mind.

Pearl and Earl

Founded in 2007, Pearl and Earl is the creation of designer Jacqui Pearce, who has a passion for creating bright and beautiful things. Over the years, Jacqui and her husband, Gareth Horton, have developed a range of personalised homeware, graphic prints and original partyware, with a focus on sourcing exclusive and original designs.

Sophia Victoria Joy

Sophia Victoria Joy was founded in 2010 by Sophia, who runs the family business, creating personalised gifts with thoughtful wrapping and trimmings, from her Hampshire-based studio. She now has a specially selected team of people working behind the scenes to ensure that every product made is just as special as the original concept she once dreamed up over a cup of tea. The business continues to grow through Sophia's vision and determination.

A Piece Of

The symmetrically named business partners Anna and Anna created A Piece Of in 2008 with a range of personalised prints designed to add a touch of colour and humour to every home. Over the years, they've moved into printing T-shirts and other homewares, and continue to expand their designs based on their success.

Delightful Living

Anne Hyde is a trained signmaker and created Delightful Living with her husband Paul to offer bespoke signs for all sorts of occasions. They have a particular niche in weddings and have built on this to offer unique wedding styling. Based in rural Derbyshire, the business has grown and expanded to include homewares and a collection for children.

A QUICK-REFERENCE GUIDE

Take some time to get familiar with the practical exercises you need to complete in the next thirty days. We know you can struggle to allow yourself time to concentrate on you, but this is time worth investing. You do not always have to complete each exercise in one go – break them up if needed, but do complete each exercise before moving on to the next. It also helps that sometimes a task requires you simply to sit and think. Everyone can wait! Leave the washing, forget about tidying the stock room, let the children watch some TV ... It's time for you and only you.

The 30-Day Plan

4	5	6
THE BREAK THROUGH QUIZ *allow*: three hours ☐	**KSI – KNOCKOUT SELF - INTRODUCTION** *allow*: one hour ☐	**VISUALISATION** *allow*: 15–20 minutes ☐

11		13
HOW TO IDENTIFY THE REASONS WHY AND THE WAYS IN WHICH YOU ARE CONFIDENT *allow*: across two days – thinking time is important here – clear spaces (where you can) in your working day ☐		**CONFIDENCE IN ACTION – LEADERSHIP** *allow*: two hours ☐

18	19	20
LEARN THE LANGUAGE OF MONEY *allow*: two hours ☐	**KNOW YOUR CUSTOMER** *allow*: bite-sized periods of time over two days	☐

25	26	27
ELIMINATE VERBAL GRAFFITI *allow*: ongoing across a day, while carrying on as normal ☐	**BE INTERVIEW-READY** *allow*: three hours ☐	**AUDIT YOUR SUPPORT NETWORK** *allow*: thirty minutes ☐

Start here

1 WRITE YOUR OWN HONESTY DIARIES *allow:* two hours ☐	**2** ASSESSING YOUR WORKING DAY *allow:* ten minutes at the end of three working days ☐	**3** YOUR (HONEST) LIFE IN COLOUR *allow:* one hour ☐
7 SETTING YOUR 30-DAY OBJECTIVES *allow:* two hours ☐	**8** GET YOUR HR HOUSE IN ORDER *allow:* one day ☐	**9** **10** BE YOUR OWN COACH FOR A DAY *allow:* one and a half days ☐
14 THE CONFIDENCE TEST *allow:* two hours ☐	**15** SET OUT YOUR END GOAL *allow:* two hours ☐	**16** **17** FINANCIAL FORECASTING *allow:* one and a half days ☐
21 DEFINE YOUR CUSTOMER EXPERIENCE *allow:* one hour ☐	**22** REVIEW YOUR CUSTOMER SERVICE *allow:* three hours ☐	**23** SCHEDULED FITNESS *allow:* ten minutes THE WARDROBE AUDIT *allow:* three hours (then shopping!) ☐ **24** BE RSVP-READY *allow:* one hour WATCH YOURSELF BACK *allow:* three hours ☐
28 DO NOTHING! *allow:* a whole day...! ☐	**29** THE ANNUAL REVIEW *allow:* one hour ☐	**30** THE 30-DAY REVIEW *allow:* two hours ☐ *Finished!*

Hello

The story of us:
Holly, Sophie and
notonthehighstreet.com

'This suspense is terrible. Let's hope it will last.'

OSCAR WILDE

This book is all about you, it really is. We know that you are pretty marvellous already – the mere act of picking this book up off the shelf shows great instinct and taste – but we want to guide you towards being an even better you. A better you, one that is mentally and physically in good shape, will mean that your business improves too. We also know that to take your business to the next level means changing your mindset in terms of your expectations and ambitions. When you have spent a long time just trying to get a business off the ground or getting the job you want, you may be too afraid or weary to think much further ahead. But we want you to start planning how to double your turnover or become CEO of the company you work for. We want you to both plan for and expect success. To do that you may need to bolster your confidence, change the way you look at things and get comfortable with high-level business talk. That's what we're here for, and, by the end of *Shape Up Your Business*, we believe you will be ready for the next step – and beyond. Whether it's growth, expansion, promotion or significant investment, we want you to get to the next level and we'll give you the tools to achieve it.

But before we do that, we thought we'd better explain why we think we're the right people to help. So that's what this chapter is about. Who we are, where we are – and why that's good for you.

(NB Those readers who have read our first book will see a little familiar ground covered in our early years but, don't worry, there's plenty of fresh new stuff to tell you when it comes to the business. Hold tight.)

our story

Holly's story

I was born in 1977 to driven, successful parents so perhaps it was no surprise that by six years old I was not only earning my pocket money by doing jobs around the house but was asking for better-paid ones. My dad, Robert, worked for Apple Records with The Beatles and my mum, Sally, whose own mother was a French entrepreneur, worked for Janet Street-Porter. When I was seven, we moved to Holland where I went to international schools: my best friends were Brazilian, Irish and Japanese and I learned to speak in German, French, Dutch and English. That kind of education was invaluable, teaching me that people can do things differently, not necessarily better or worse. It means I'm always open to new ideas but equally, I don't believe in the impossible – I just think you have to look at a problem in a different way.

When I was a young teenager, we came back home to Chiswick, London, and it wasn't long before I'd got myself a job cleaning a pub. At weekends I worked as a silver-service waitress and I even ran the school tuck shop. At sixteen years old, I took a work-experience opportunity at Publicis, the advertising agency – I was already eager to get started on a career. For the next three summers I worked there my entire holidays. It meant a long commute each way, every day, and more than once it crossed my mind that my friends were all having a more relaxing time in the sunshine, but I stuck to it. Finally, on the morning that my A-level results came in, I had an interview with Rick Bendel, then chief executive of Publicis, who offered me a job as a junior account executive. I was eighteen years old. I left the interview and walked round the corner to the Peugeot 205 parked there, with my mum and sister inside, holding their breath to hear my news. We screamed with delight, drove to the school and I collected my results: Design Technology, A; Art, B; Business

Studies, E. (Who's laughing now? It's not my Business Studies teacher, that's for sure.)

Job in hand, I dropped plans to go to art school, put on my suit and went to work. It was hard. I was the youngest one there and had to prove myself. Despite a low wage – £12,000pa – I moved to a tiny flat in Harlesden, West London. But every month, when I went out for drinks with colleagues, I'd often pick up the tab and then have to wait a few weeks before I was paid back. One month I did this only to find I didn't have enough left to pay the rent. By that time, I had met Sophie – she was the account director on my team – and when she learned of this, she lent me the money. To my horror, I had no choice but to accept. I never forgot that kindness.

At twenty-one years old I was an account manager with a lot of responsibility, managing international clients and budgets of millions of pounds. I had been inspired at Publicis by my boss, Rick Bendel, the one who gave me my first break. Rick and I recently met up again and I talked with him about his career and business ethos. I was blown away to realise that we share so much in our stories. Both of us left school and started work at seventeen years old – he started at an advertising agency by offering to work for 'less than the cost of the coffee machine'; by the time he was twenty-one he was media director. At the same age I was an advertising manager, one of the youngest in London – both of us were at top-ten ad agencies. At thirty-five he was CEO of Publicis Worldwide, the first non-Frenchman to run the network. At the same age I was CEO of notonthehighstreet.com – a smaller achievement than Rick's! – but we were both doing what we wanted to do. Ten years later he became worldwide marketing director of Walmart, the largest consumer company in the world. He was one of the most successful people in retail but he told me that insecurity had always been a powerful driver for him, just as it has been for me.

Nevertheless, it's his three key principles that have also helped me succeed. Firstly: emotional insight is the key to understanding how people think. Many find it difficult to articulate how they really feel and are misunderstood. But if you show your own vulnerability, others will show theirs. If you can feel what they feel, you'll understand what their motivation and behaviour mean.

Secondly: everybody wants to feel good about themselves. Our expectations of ourselves are often unreasonable and thus our insecurities drive our actions. I have learned in business it is more vital to understand why your customers love you than to worry why some customers are rejecting you. If you stay true to the reasons you are great then loyalty will be your reward.

Finally: simplicity is divinity. The best solutions are the simplest and common sense is often the answer to complex problems; those executed well endure the test of time. I am not a technical person so I know that if something makes sense to me it will make sense to everybody. Rick taught me all this and I couldn't be more grateful to him for it.

Back to my story ... At twenty-one I had been at Publicis for quite some time and I wanted change. I wanted to follow in the footsteps of my inspirational boss and find bigger success that I could call my own. In that same year of my milestone birthday, I married the boy I'd been with since I was fourteen years old, bought my first property and moved to work for Condé Nast, publisher of *Vogue* and *Tatler*, as a fashion ad sales manager for *Brides* magazine. From there, I was headhunted to join an online start-up, Cool White. It was a fantastic idea, showcasing luxury bridal boutiques and services, but the world – and technology – wasn't quite ready for it yet.

Two years later for no apparent reason I put on a lot of weight, very quickly – nearly four stone in as many months. After gruelling tests it was discovered that I had a brain tumour. That news alone was shattering but then the doctors told me that because of its position, they couldn't operate. We could only hope that it wouldn't grow.

I was lucky. After more hospital appointments and tests, which were probably more distressing for my husband and family than for me, we were told it wasn't malignant. But every year for the next five years I had to return to check it hadn't grown. It never did and now I'm in the clear, the chances of it growing any more are tiny.

But while it turned out okay in the end, the stress of discovering the tumour was huge. It wasn't helped by the fact that I was already aware that my marriage was in serious trouble. On top of all that, Cool White came to an end and I was out of a job. I was mature, able to act twice my age at work, but I couldn't handle my world falling apart.

Still, the mortgage payments had to be made so I set myself up as a freelance consultant, troubleshooting for ad sales teams on magazines. Quickly I was busy – busy enough not to go on holiday for two years, although I see now that I was also avoiding time to think. I had started divorce proceedings and they had turned messy.

At that point, Frank came along. I'd known him for most of my life but something suddenly changed between us. Seventeen years my senior, he gave me the courage and support I needed to believe in myself again. After just a month, he moved in with me – we knew it was quick but we also knew we were meant to be together.

Settled with Frank, my illness in remission and work ticking along, I found myself wanting to revive my creativity again, long abandoned since I dropped an art degree in favour of a job. I started making Christmas wreaths out of unusual things, such as chillies, oranges and cinnamon sticks and, pleased with the results, thought it would be nice to sell them at a craft fair. I was sure there would be one in Chiswick, where I was now living. There wasn't. So I set one up – Your Local Fair. My dad lent me £5,000 to get started; I finally repaid him a few years ago.

The first fair was in Chiswick in 2003 and the atmosphere, for me, was electric. I pulled together friends and family; they were supportive not just of the idea but because they were finally seeing their old Holly again, back in the game.

For two years, I ran Your Local Fairs all over London, fitting it around my consultancy ad sales work. Doing both meant I could hire colleagues on a freelance basis to help me with things such as website design and marketing. I even used the ad sales job as a motivator: I'd set myself a target of hitting £10,000 in revenues before I'd let myself spend thirty minutes on Your Local Fair. At the end of my first year doing this, the team I had been helping won the company's top award for sales.

The fairs were exciting and it was a fantastic feeling to be running my own business but the finances didn't work out. The success of events was very much dependent on the weather, the whims of the sporting calendar and so many other things I couldn't control and that made the cash flow unpredictable. Then in 2004 I fell pregnant, very happily so. Frank and I moved into our first home together in November of that year, I did my final fair on 16 December and Harry was born on 28 January 2005.

As a self-employed mother I had no maternity leave but the bills still had to be paid. Frank worked for the Metropolitan Police and had a steady wage but it was far from large. So when Harry was ten weeks old, I went back to work, freelancing for my old clients again, selling advertising. I put Your Local Fairs to rest.

But they wouldn't lie still. My sister, Carrie – now our head of product – was coming to the house to help me with Harry, in exchange for which I was helping her with her CV (she had just completed a degree in psychology with ergonomics). I kept saying to her: 'I just can't get this idea – giving small businesses a platform – out of my mind.' I had discovered so many of them with fantastic products to sell. I knew now that fairs were not the answer but I knew those sellers needed *something*. Perhaps an online directory would be the solution?

For a few months I kept selling advertising. I'd push Harry down the hall in his baby walker and he would slowly, very slowly, work his way back to me. By that time, I'd have closed a deal. Then I'd push him back again.

All the while, I kept picking at my idea. How could I put Your Local Fair online? What would make it work? One thing I knew for certain – I couldn't do it by myself. I had to find the right person who could be strong where I knew I was weak. I went through all the people I knew but my mind always kept going back to Sophie.

At first, I wasn't entirely sure why this would be. We had been friends at work and kept in touch over the years, with a coffee or lunch every twelve months or so. But she was older, had two young children, was trying to get a business of her own off the ground and her life had probably moved on. I didn't think she could possibly be interested. Carrie kept pestering me: 'Have you emailed Sophie yet?' Eventually, I wrote to her.

Ultimately, I knew she was the right person and not just because she had been so kind to me in the past. I knew I needed her yin to my yang. I'm driven and can always see the big picture but I'm not so hot on the detail. Plus, I knew she had maturity and I'd already seen her in action, being impressive in meetings. She could stand up to people and has an incredibly precise mind.

Within twenty-four hours Sophie had written back.

She was interested.

Sophie's story

My childhood was chaotic but happy. I was born in 1965, the second of four sisters, to two rather extraordinary parents. My mother is Penny Vincenzi, a journalist and bestselling novelist; my father, Paul, ran his own businesses, later became an inventor and was always a brave risk-taker when it came to his career. School never appealed much to me, though I applied myself to the subjects I liked or knew mattered, and by the time I finally finished with education I'd gone to eight different schools. As a girl of ten, I preferred to play offices, poring over the magazine *Girl About Town* to see what jobs there were, working out how much I would have to earn so that I could buy my own flat.

I wasn't interested in going to university – the state of my sister's digs was enough to put me off – and work looked exciting. I used to spend my school holidays hanging out in (for which read, tidying up) the fashion cupboard at my mum's office when she was features editor for the iconic *Honey* magazine. Immediately I could throw away my school uniform, I heard about an opening at Hearst Magazines and, thanks to a friend of my mum's putting in a word with the health and beauty editor for me, I got an interview and then, thrillingly, the job – editorial assistant for *Cosmopolitan* magazine.

Highly aware that my connections and youth meant I had to be twice as good as anyone might expect of me, I spent my time there half terrified, half in awe. The women who ran the magazine at that time in the mid-1980s were pioneers in their field, placing as much emphasis on money, success and self-reliance as they did on sex, fashion and beauty in the *Cosmo* pages. At nineteen years old I got my first by-line and many more followed. I revelled in an atmosphere that was alive with energy and commitment to producing the best possible work. I learned to write to be interesting, not for an essay grade. What's more I got to spend time learning from some of the best photographers, stylists, models, make-up artists, art directors and graphic designers in the business.

Looking back, I see that the influence this job had on my life was huge. The women I worked with there inspired me to be professional, fair and to strive for the highest standards throughout my entire career. I might have been a little green and impressionable – though I remember carrying lots of my teenage cynicism into my twenties! – but it seemed to me that they had it just right. There was the highest concentration I have ever since seen of women who mentored the juniors, were unafraid to share the credit, were clever and talented and – this is the part I recall over and over again – worked seamlessly and really quite elegantly as a team. To work in a good magazine editorial office is to witness process at its very best. Everyone knows exactly what they and everyone else should be doing, when and in what order, respects their expertise, gives them space to get it done and done well. So many of them went on to great success, to being the firsts in their field in Fleet Street, in the cosmetics industry, in publishing.

It wasn't all sunshine and roses though. Half the time I was absolutely terrified. These women were scary, grown up, looked amazing and I made mistakes. There was, without question, a *Devil Wears Prada* vibe going on, and I also tried to learn there how to be demanding of my staff, to expect the very best, without frightening the hell out of them!

After climbing to the dizzy heights of beauty writer, I moved across to *Good Housekeeping* magazine as a health and beauty editor. At twenty years old I'd got a mortgage and bought my first flat, just as I'd planned to as a little girl. More confident in my abilities by now, I thoroughly enjoyed myself when it came to the writing, journalism and photographic styling. Yet, I noticed even then that it was the consumer elements I really thrived on, discovering new brands for the shopping pages. Increasingly, I began to feel that it was this area that could create new challenges more stimulating than publishing. There was a business itch that was starting to get under my skin.

That was when I was offered the chance to work for Barbara Attenborough Associates as a creative brand manager on Boots No7 and 17 cosmetic accounts, focusing on seasonal colours and new products. I leapt at it. Not only would I, by now a twenty-four-year-old with a healthy interest in looking good, have fun spending all day dreaming up new make-up colours, packaging and names but that business itch could get scratched. Barbara was an impressive person but in a very different way from those at *Cosmo*. She was a founder, yes, and a highly successful businesswoman, but also a mother, a groundbreaker, the first woman ever on the board of The Boots Company PLC. She was generous and nurturing in an altogether warmer way, took me under her wing, was able to operate however she wanted and I sussed out quickly that she had become both powerful and independent, able to be her own person by having her own successful company. That was very formative.

In my mid-twenties, perhaps feeling that student urge after all, I decided to take time out for a year to live in Sydney and take a round-the-world trip. I got a new buzz – finding cool stuff from different corners of the globe and packing it up and sending it home. I came home ready to launch myself more definitively in the business world and decided that advertising made the most sense of my experience to date. I started with the small but hot GGK London and loved working there – an of-the-moment creative agency where we won more awards than we knew what to do with.

But I wanted success, the kind that gives you control over your fate, and I knew I had to work in a big agency with big beauty accounts if I was to climb the ladder. I moved to Publicis, to manage campaigns for big brands, from George at Asda to L'Oréal. It was a great agency but somehow it was never the perfect fit for me. It felt large and institutional and gave me my first insider's view of the power play that went on in corporate politics. More than ever, I longed to do my own thing and worked in the evenings on a novel – an advertising thriller – that I was convinced would do the trick of propelling me out of there.

There were, however, two very good outcomes from my time at Publicis. First of all, I met Holly, who came to work with me as a young exec. She was instantly and obviously exceptional. In all the best ways, she reminded me of the people I'd worked with in magazines and admired so much: energetic, creative, dynamic and confident. We got on very well immediately and I only got fonder of her as I watched her rapid climb through the ranks.

Secondly, it was during that time I met Simon, now my husband. Meeting him was a major turning point for all the obvious reasons and also for others less so. As you might not expect from a man, and a City broker at that, Simon turned out to be on what we have come to call 'the quest' for the perfect item. We spent our courtship in The Conran Shop and flea markets, and travelled all over the world, finding vintage and retro things for our house. It's Simon who cooks our delicious and stylish suppers when friends come round. Exploring that world with him was very exciting.

Not long after Holly had joined the team at Publicis, I became pregnant with Ollie, my first (now seventeen years old). When he was five months old I went back to work and then a year later, I was pregnant with Honor (now fifteen). With two tiny children at home, I wanted an alternative to the fifty-hour working weeks and the long daily commute, so in 1999 I left the company.

Holly and I kept in touch. I was always anxious to know that she was doing okay, particularly when times got tough for her, but we did essentially go our separate ways. I was now preoccupied with raising my children and yet not letting go of my career ambitions. For a while, I patched things together with consultancy and freelance work, writing for magazines about style and shopping – which gave me an insight into trends and what people were looking for – and a book about weddings. I also joined a dotcom start-up, giving me a head start in the e-commerce arena. But as I approached my late thirties, I started to see how expensive life was. Making money was something I *had* to do – it was time to take control.

With my friend Nicki Marsh, I set up a small business styling private and corporate events and from there took a course in floristry. I started making huge, gorgeous door wreaths one Christmas, selling them at shopping fairs – not knowing that Holly was having the same idea at the same time! – and learned two things. Firstly, that making money through flowers was hard, flowers being perishable, expensive, fluctuating massively in price and a nightmare to store, not to mention the routine 3am starts. And secondly, that selling through shopping fairs is a tough way to earn a living – and I only did it for a few months. But I had found a gap in the market. There was a need for things for the home that were funky, original and artisan. Despite the challenges of doing this with flowers, I was up for it. I wanted – needed – a big challenge.

Then, in one week in 2005, my destiny changed. Just as I had decided to take the leap and move up a gear with the floristry, I finally got an agent to take on the novel, realised it was now or never with a third baby and I opened an email from Holly asking if I might be interested in going into business with her ...

TOGETHER AT LAST

The timing was perfect. We needed each other, we needed the challenge and, best of all, the world needed us. The days when looking good was all about wearing the biggest designer label you could afford were dying out. We both knew that people were increasingly seeking out things for their home that were original and authentic. And we knew that people were out there making these things, brilliantly. The problem was that they didn't know how to find each other. Until we came along.

Within a day or so we had met up and begun work, starting off in each other's houses at our kitchen tables. From the beginning we worked long hours, propelled by an unshakeable belief that we had something that could succeed. We knew there was a gap in the market, thanks to the fairs and our insight into consumer trends. And we knew that online was the way to go. At first, we were simply going to provide a directory of makers and sellers but it wasn't long before we realised that a transactional site, while more technically complex and challenging, was the future for us and our potential customers: one shopping basket, lots of people selling, which is the essence of our notonthehighstreet.com brand.

We also came to realise that the dynamic of the two of us was what was going to make this business work. Between us we could create a company that had in its leadership vision, creativity, presence and confidence, together with a rigorous eye for detail and structure. We wrote many business plans, bringing together our ambitious financial forecasts, negotiating skills and careful research, all accurately and meticulously presented. This ultimately meant that if we did something impulsive or inventive, there was structure, form and protocol there too. What we absolutely shared were our extremely high standards. From the off we had an unbudging refusal to be anything but completely slick and professional.

Despite this, we were careful and deliberate about the way in which we approached our business partnership (we already knew we were good friends and colleagues). We both filled out a long and detailed questionnaire, which we then swapped and read, clarifying exactly how we both felt about our visions for the company, the time we could give it and our attitudes. We'd recommend anyone else planning to go into a partnership to do the same.

Later that year, in 2005, we went out to persuade our first partners (those small businesses we work with) to join. We were fairly certain that we would be tapping into a rich vein but it was only when Holly spent the day calling potential partners to see if it really would sell that we realised we were on to something big. Every single one of them said yes.

Before we could build on this, we had to raise funds. We were not the kind of people to have money lying around, nor were our families. We begged, borrowed and raided our small savings. Frank even gave us the compensation money he had spent six years fighting for from the Metropolitan Police, for damage to his hearing. We squeezed everything so much that our mortgage payments could barely be made – any more and our houses would have been at risk.

That should have scared the hell out of us and yet, somehow, we weren't frightened. We believed so utterly and completely in what we were doing that we felt only excitement. Perhaps that's just us, or perhaps it was down to the strength of the idea, but we always knew it would come right in the end.

Still, not everyone was jumping on board our ship. There were partners who said no, there were banks that wouldn't give us loans, there were investors who felt they couldn't back us. Back then, it seemed highly improbable that consumers would pay for goods that historically they needed to touch and feel first. It was only a few years ago but even the internet behemoths such as Amazon and eBay were not nearly the size they are now. Only Natalie Massenet's Net-A-Porter could provide proof that people were prepared to buy luxury goods online.

We ploughed on. Anyone who said no to us had their name written on a piece of paper and posted into the 'You'll Be Sorry' box. We became insanely propelled to succeed by these rejections. So perhaps we should thank them. (Or maybe not.)

Less than a year after we had agreed to work together, in January 2006, we moved into our first offices. The unglamorous, breeze-block walls of Aaron House in Richmond. The first day had just us, Carrie and Louise Cullen (a friend of Carrie's – keen, sharp and best of all, available). Two weeks later, crazily and masochistically, we put up a microsite online and named a date for launch: 3 April 2006. Just over two months away.

What started as a fun idea came to torment and terrorise us as the clock counted down the days and we found ourselves time-bound to a promise made to the press and our sellers. Sellers who had, moreover, handed over their cash in the form of a signing-up fee, with the promise that they'd be making it back in sales through us. But as we got nearer and nearer the date, we realised that the agency we had hired to build our site wasn't going to be able to do it. They batted away our concerns and we were only too quick to repress what we knew in our heart of hearts: it wasn't going to happen on time.

All the while, we had been building our team, mainly from friends and family, many of whom stayed with us for years. We roped in several more when we needed the extra help – there were days when we'd have sixteen people sitting on the floor with laptops. We'd look at them, count them, multiply that number by the hourly wage we'd have to pay them and tried not to be sick.

The day after April Fools' Day we realised the joke was on us. We were doomed. The site wasn't going to be transactional on launch day – the next day. We were launching a brand-new, all-singing-and-dancing, revolutionary shopping website on which no one would be able to buy a single thing.

So we spun it. We called it a preview and asked everyone who visited to come back later. We also invited them to register on the site in a competition to win money to spend with us another day. To our incredulity, it worked. Sixteen thousand people visited and most of them, it seemed, entered the competition. Our email inbox scrolled over and over for hours, looking as if it had gone out of control like some scene from a movie.

In the end we relaunched the site twice and it was transactional a week later. We rebuilt our site in secret, thanks to the wizardry of our yet-to-be technical director Joe Simms (a university friend of Louise's, he popped in to help us resize some images one day and stayed with us for five years), then fired the agency. The pressure of those early days – the building, the near crash, the rescue, the final launch – was almost geological in its intensity. We grew up, fast. And we still had a lot to learn.

Two things kept us going: the belief that we were doing something so right and the responsibility to the people we had signed up. We call the sellers on our site *partners* because we work with them, not for them, and they work with us, not for us. We provide them with a beautiful storefront, technical support, marketing, business support and hundreds of thousands of potential consumers. We get a kick out of knowing that we are helping real people with real skills. We're enabling them to grow their businesses as well as providing consumers with amazing products, responsibly produced. But that brings a huge responsibility: livelihoods depend on us not just surviving but getting it right, and growing.

Alongside that, our business model demands that it be big. Our income comes from commissions on sales, but after costs only a slither of commission is left, so we need lots of sales to make enough revenue. But to make lots of sales means we need more partners and each time we gain a partner we also gain new costs in order to include and support them. Money to market them, acquire more customers and develop ever more features on the website. In other words, as we grew bigger and more successful our costs went soaring up – further than we could predict. Further than we could afford.

But it took us a while to realise this. A few months in we were beginning to feel that we had nailed it. More and more customers were coming to the site and buying. Partners were signing up. We got masses of positive press in newspapers and magazines. There was a buzz and we were making honey. It was at that exact moment, just as we were coasting on a wave of blissful complacency that things were going our way, that we came within weeks of losing everything we had put into the business, and a lot more besides.

For the first six months we hadn't paid ourselves a penny but we worked fifteen-hour days as well as every weekend. We were ecstatic to be running our own business but we were also permanently exhausted, hadn't seen our friends for months and barely saw our families. We'd pulled in favours from everyone we knew and our nearest and dearest were watching to see how we fared. We wanted and needed this to work.

But the cash flow was sporadic. Not only did we have to put money upfront to accommodate the growth but expensive things would go wrong at a moment's notice. There were one or two times when we'd lock ourselves in the meeting room for a good cry, hoping the team wouldn't notice our red-rimmed eyes when we came out. Without additional funding, we were going to implode and it wouldn't be pretty.

Even in these dire straits, we turned business away – £1 million worth to be precise, in the first year alone – companies who applied to sell with us but who were not in the 10 per cent we knew would succeed and deliver on the style and promise of our notonthehighstreet.com brand.

The bottom line, however, was disappearing from view. Around the summer of 2006, having launched the previous April, alarm bells started to ring. We didn't so much not hear them as feel confident they would stop. Suddenly, in October, we hit a wall. It became apparent that if we didn't find a life-saving injection of cash, our business dream was going to die a gruesome death and quite possibly our hard-earned professional reputations with it.

When we finally looked at the figures we came to the startling realisation that we had just enough money to keep the business going until Christmas, at which point we would have to shut it down. That was the sting in the tail – we knew sales would thrive over the festive period (and they did) but it wouldn't be enough.

We had nowhere to turn. Our families could loan us no more: Robert had spent the last of his savings on us; Sophie's parents had given all they could. The banks wouldn't help unless we gave them our houses as security. (No way.)

We went metaphorically scrabbling down the back of the sofa again. We called anyone we knew who had more than a few quid to their name to see if they'd be willing to invest. We asked everyone we knew to ask everyone they knew if they knew anyone who might be willing to invest. We hoped and prayed that if we threw enough mud at the wall, some of it might stick. We needed a miracle.

We got one.

After a dispiriting day when the gods truly seemed to be against us – an investor who was going to back us went bust themselves – our long-time friend and consultant PR director Julie Turner was chatting to a well-connected entrepreneur in church, asking them if they might know anyone who would be interested in investing in us. Yes, they said, they might.

That person turned out to be Tom Teichman of SPARK Ventures, the man who wrote the first cheque for the founders of lastminute.com. Always looking for the next idea, he gave us a meeting. We presented as if our lives depended on it – well, they probably did. Afterwards, Tom and his team thanked us, said goodbye and left the room – they had another meeting to get to. Feeling lonely and pathetic, we packed away our samples with as much dignity and haste as bulky customised doorstops and witty T-shirts will allow. Robert gave us each a little smile, trying and failing to rouse our hopes. We made for the door.

In the corridor was Tom. He beckoned us back into the room. 'I've just had a chat with the team,' he said. 'We're going to do it. We think you've got that spark. We'll talk tomorrow.'

We'd done it. We still had more heart-stopping moments to come. Our attempts to raise money had shaped up our business hugely – we'd always tried to be as professional as possible – but seeking funds from a venture capitalist meant everything had to be as shiny as a corporal's shoes, from our legal requirements to a monthly reporting system and the overall business model. And now that they had said yes, we had to go through due diligence and contract negotiations – we were giving them equity and a place on the board in return for their investment – fastidiously producing market reports, references and financial projections for weeks and weeks. In the nick of time, SPARK came through, delivering our first chunk of funds on Valentine's Day 2007. It was the start of a romantic affair that ended only in 2013 when the time was right for them to reap the very substantial rewards of their original investment to help other new businesses.

SHAPING UP OUR BUSINESS

Since then we have gone out several times for a new round of investment and each time it's still fairly full on – if the money doesn't come in then we might not grow and scale in the way we need to – but each time that investment has made the difference it was designed to do. From the original 100 partners we had signed up on launch day, we now have 5,000. In 2013, seven of our partners hit a point where they had turned over a million pounds in a year. Last year, our average annual growth rate since the business launched reached 151 per cent to the end of 2013. Since our launch to the middle of 2014, we have injected £200 million into the UK economy with our platform for small businesses. Our customers are growing too, with a marketing database of 2 million people; we are predicted to be in the top 100 most visited sites in Britain, sitting above British Airways and Sainsbury's.

But all this doesn't mean it's an easy job now.

Holly: 'I am petrified most of the time if the truth be told, despite the successes we have had and the size of our operation. Actually the more people that are employed and the more partners that are supported, the more weight on my shoulders.

'A few years ago we were close to finalising a very important deal. I had a great feeling about it and knew that it would be better than the last few times we had gone out fundraising. How could it not? We were bigger, more successful and stronger generally. I was stronger, too.

'I was the one who was managing the deal and I had never done anything like it in my life. It felt like climbing a mountain in a bikini. At one stage, the deal was resting on one of the three calls I had a day with the other party (any time of night or day).

'The deal was fast, just a three-month turnaround, but two weeks before we were due to close I got the call that meant the deal was very much at risk. I felt as if the business, the partners' futures, Sophie's and my and our close family's dreams had just fallen hard on to me. I remember a sudden wail of pure pain (when I had put down the phone – just!). I am sure the whole office thought someone had died.

'Better times were to come – more of this in the Confidence chapter – but I will never forget that moment. And it taught me a great deal – that the fear stays. I felt as if I gained a decade of experience in those few short months. But learn to know yourself better and better and then the fear can almost become your friend.'

While our brand is still true to its original essence, the structure of the business itself is beyond recognition. Where we started as Holly and Sophie, running our start-up as best we could, now we are CEO and Director, with a board of non-executive directors. Where before we had someone on a laptop on the floor, now we have entire departments and a senior management team to run them. We have 200 employees. We've moved from the breeze blocks of Aaron House and next we will have a new 35,000 sq ft headquarters in Richmond, resplendent with out-of-the-ordinary, on-brand styling and polished meeting rooms that we'll continue to name after the cafes that served us so well as meeting rooms in the early days (Orange Pekoe, Treehouse).

And while we are still Holly and Sophie – why wouldn't we be? – sitting with friends and family, being teased or laughing at the usual jokes, as businesswomen we *have* changed. We are no longer just trying to survive but we are learning to conquer our fears and look forward to the future. That doesn't mean we don't stop learning – we constantly revisit, evaluate, improve, tweak and grow with the business. A company is a living organism; it needs to be continuously nurtured, fed and watered. What we have got now is experience and we've learned what nourishes us as leaders and in turn the business and that's what we'd like this book to do for you. To help you now and in the future – you can return to this book whenever you feel stuck and need help for you and your business or career to move up again.

We learned that we had to change if the business was going to grow. As we became better businesswomen, inside and out, the business got better too. That's what we want for you. We've realised that if you're going to make that change – from survivor to torchbearer – you have to create the capacity to change. It's not just about inner hunger (though that sure helps) but about adjusting your attitude to risk; about clearing your house out, both mentally and physically, to allow the new to come in. It's about confidence, knowing who you are and bringing out the very best of yourself to negotiate the very best future for you and your business.

WHERE WE ARE NOW

So if you think we sailed off into the sunset after SPARK Ventures came through – think again. Growing a business, particularly at the pace we had to do it, is hard. And we made mistakes. We had to learn a lot – *a lot!* – about how to run and work with our technical team. There were moments when building a company felt too difficult, too dark, too hard. We couldn't always see the payoff, let alone the payday. We had to learn how to fall in love with our business again – and we did but it's not the dizzy madness of the first time; it comes around the second and third times with experience and the knowledge that you can accept your love with all its flaws but only because you have the confidence to conduct that relationship on your own terms.

Holly: 'At every stage, you learn to get comfortable with that level. Yet every next landing you reach seems to have another never-ending staircase ahead. I find now that my expectations read almost seamlessly and subconsciously so that as I hit the level I've been working so hard to get to, I hardly even notice. I only see the next one I need to reach.

'Part of that, too, I think is that you never fully let go of the start-up mentality. We got burned in those early days. When at last we moved into new headquarters, there was no sense of, 'Oh, yes, *of course.*' I absolutely felt: 'Wow! We've hit the big time!' and it was a great feeling. But I also wasn't going to forget how much rent we now had to pay. The driving motivation I had at the very start was still there.'

Working with a board of directors, as opposed to just the two of us sitting in a small room, is actually a lot like being promoted in a corporation. With it comes a lot of responsibility and accountability. From one day to the next, you're running with the power players. You have to do what it takes to keep up and keep your eye on the finish line. That's what we're here for. It took us seven years to learn how to do it. We hope you can do it in thirty days.

WE ASKED OUR PARTNERS

How does the reality of running your own company compare with what you expected? What is the thing that is most different to how you envisaged? Is anything just how you pictured it?

My 1st Years: It's better than I could ever have imagined. My destiny is in my hands and the business grows as we want it to grow and when we want it to grow. I used to be scared of mistakes and failures, but now I embrace them (in moderation) as it lets me learn that much more as an individual and then I will not make the same mistakes again. But it is all amazing!

Oakdene Designs: Running my own company is great, it's a lot of fun and creates a lot of unique challenges every day. At the moment I am having to put more time into manufacture than I had anticipated. I have many more staff than I thought I would and we have grown faster than I ever expected. I was never too sure of where this business would take me and even now I wouldn't be able to guess where the business will be next year. I didn't envisage ever being able to produce the quantity of orders that we do now; our record is completing an order every sixty-seven seconds over a full eight-hour day.

Ellie Ellie: It's all happened so fast and my reality has overtaken my expectations. In my mind my plans only took me as far as running my business full time, then before I knew it the company was limited, VAT registered with seven members of staff, add in a mixture of lots of hard work, blood, sweat and tears. This does of course mean my job has significantly changed throughout the years, having started doing everything myself from designing, marketing, photography, accounts, dispatching and customer service, I have slowly handed over responsibility, which has led my job to becoming more business orientated than expected but I love it. It's my business and I know it inside out, upside down and this is what I am good at. My main expectation and goal when setting up my own business was to create a job I loved. I found a little saying back when I was first starting up which read 'Do what you love and love what you do' and it's this saying that I still use continually to focus my work and keep me motivated today. Starting a business wasn't just about making money for me, it was about making sure I woke up every morning knowing I was going to a job I loved.

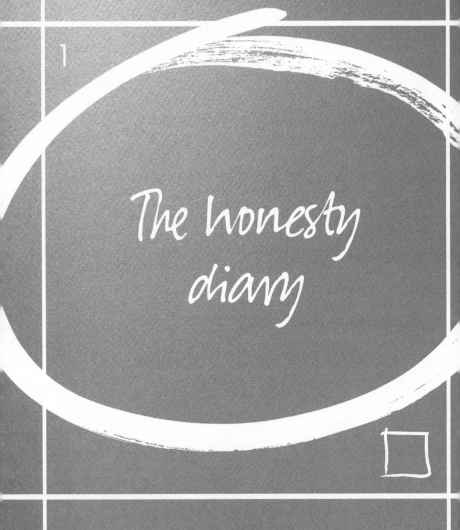

1

The honesty diary

'The truth will set you free, but first it will piss you off.'
GLORIA STEINEM

DAYS 1 TO 5

Pinpointing where your strengths and weaknesses
lie to make you a better leader; improving your
working day and time management

We hope you've seen from the previous chapter that we have been as honest as we can be with you, our reader, about both how difficult and how wonderful building notonthehighstreet.com has been for us. We know that many business leaders might advise a rather more polished picture but we are not afraid to present ourselves as we really are because we have learned an important thing over the years: being honest about who you are – both at home and at work – is the quickest, simplest route to becoming the best you can be. We have faced some hard truths about ourselves and how we have grown with the business but the result has been, we hope, that we are better leaders. This chapter will help you achieve this too.

As you take your business up to the next level, the stakes get higher. We know now that if we don't speak up and say we don't agree with, for example, the strategy for our next catalogue, then a mistake could cost us millions of pounds. Not being honest, with yourself or others, is often little more than a habit but we're here to help you break it. Telling the truth doesn't always have to be harsh – you can be fair; you simply have to respect time and money as the lifeblood of your business.

achieving
clarity

In identifying your own abilities and weak spots, as well as those of the people you work with, you'll be a better leader. You'll communicate with greater clarity; everyone will understand what it is they have to do and be able to do it and there won't be any grey areas that determine how your business performs.

Suppose you wrongly assign a task to someone and deep down you know this but do not admit it. You will spend months coaching them, changing the task itself, trying to take on some of the jobs yourself. They end up losing confidence, are unhappy and confused, when all the while they could be doing something different that they would be brilliant at. If only you had said: 'I'm going to reassign this task to someone else.'

Or suppose you are not honest about your reasons for a decision, so that no one else can really understand it, let alone support it, buy into it and help you make it happen. If you do it differently, tell people exactly what's happening and why and deal with the questions upfront (even sensitive things are better addressed in a straightforward manner), you will have a far stronger bond between your team and your goal. We have discovered this for ourselves time and again.

Doing this isn't always hard – it can be a real pleasure to discover that it is in fact the things that you most love to do, the things that inspire you best that will drive you further forward in your career than you ever thought possible. We hope the practical exercises are fun, as well as revealing. Sometimes it's not always about overcoming challenges but about embracing and using the things you love to push ahead.

FIRST THINGS FIRST

The first honest question we asked ourselves was: what do we need to be honest about? Have we been honest with ourselves and each other about our strengths and weaknesses? Have we admitted that it's okay *not* to be good at everything, so long as you can rely on someone who is, improving your skills along the way? Are we honestly using our time well? We both know it's too easy to work through the to-do list or sit through a meeting without thinking about how necessary or important each task is. And have we been honest about what, or who, is in the way? We call these our blockers – you have to recognise them and call them out, because they rarely disappear of their own accord.

We try to acknowledge when we're avoiding certain tasks that need to be completed for the business, or if we haven't had a truly honest and essential conversation with a colleague, or if we didn't ask others to be honest with us. Acknowledgement is the first and hardest step. After that, working out what to do, then making it happen – even if these can be rather painful at times – are the two elements you need to achieve. And then when you've addressed something honestly – this is the great part you can never quite imagine when you're worried sick about something – you feel better. *Much* better.

Both of us have come to realise that being honest with ourselves about what is slowing us down means we have to find a way of getting it to the top of our list and be forced to tackle it. We each have our own way of doing this.

Sophie: 'When something really tricky is hanging over me at work that I haven't dealt with, I actually feel quite flat, quite often before I realise what it is I need to face. It slows me down, physically and mentally. When I recognise that feeling, I make myself stop, work out what it is, it's not always obvious, and write it on a big orange sticker and stick it up on my kitchen wall next to the kettle, so that it's the first thing I see before I even get to my desk. Then I know I've got to deal with it – or it's going to be my morning wake-up call for evermore – and I do.'

Holly: 'Something I am trying to embrace in my daily life is to tackle something difficult every day. Sounds exhausting but slowly it is working. It's taken a while for me to embrace this but I've come to see just how much baggage one carries around and how it brings down your working day. I have a list and I add to it and sometimes I leave the hardest issues for months but it does all get done. I am starting to feel freer and freer day by day. I decided this had to be a daily task in order to get real momentum. Of course, life has a habit of never allowing you to have a list with everything ticked off!'

Most importantly, we need to be honest about our drivers. Why are we here, doing this – both day to day and in the bigger picture? Holly's only happy if her '9 to 5' is about big leaps and dramatic change, constantly pushing the business and herself forward – and she'll endure a grim day so long as it gets her there. Sophie's more inclined to seek satisfaction and pride in her work and that of the team, knowing that even if it sometimes doesn't show immediate results, it's one route to the most exceptional outcomes. Being exceptional is one of the things we value most in our business. We can afford those differences because we're a team, but if you're going it alone, be honest. Do you have both those bases – aggressive pace and high standards – covered?

DIARIES

First off, to see the overall picture of what's happening when, where and for how long, we looked at our diaries. Not the ones the Sunday supplements like to publish, where business leaders are up at 9am for a breakfast of home-made granola with a picture-perfect family, before floating into the office to solve the world's problems and rounding off the day with a session of yoga. Hmm. No, our days are a little more, er, chaotic than that. A little more, we'd like to think, based in reality, even if that reality is exhausting.

So, these are our honesty diaries. We've each done a different format, to bring out different elements of our working and home lives. There's no such thing as a typical day for either of us but these are snapshots of our time at notonthehighstreet.com HQ.

HOLLY'S HONESTY DIARY – A TYPICAL DAY

6.30–7am Rise and shine, if not earlier – my son, Harry, has never been able to wait to get out of bed and now we've been joined by a puppy …

7–8am This is meant to be a strict Harry hour – uniform, chats, breakfast, talking about what we are going to achieve today. But the reality is: I'm getting dressed, doing my make-up and looking at my iPhone (my PA emails me my list for the day). Frank and I also have a mission control book for the family, in which we can make notes about what needs to be tackled, whether it's Harry's vegetable consumption or that we need to think about a break. It's our solution for keeping us both close to the family mechanics, without having to have a sticky conversation in the middle of getting our son dressed. But all of this has to be done invisibly because Harry needs to feel that this is his time.

8–8.30am Walk, bike or take bus to work, depending on what I need to do that day.

8.30–9am Settle into the office. Get my first cup of coffee.

9am–6pm I'm in a meeting. I'm in meetings on the hour, every hour, throughout every working day. An hour is pencilled in for lunch but not because I go out, simply because meetings always run over and that gives us the leeway. I have between seven and nine meetings a day.

Every two weeks or so I have a mini-meltdown and work from home for half a day. This is when I do the things I really enjoy and I'll save them up for this time. It relieves the pressure, means I can spend a few hours thinking and planning, getting a couple of new projects under way and do something for the longer-term future of the company.

6–6.30pm I sit down with Victoria, my PA, to go over the following day. She gives me a red folder, like the Queen's red box, and in that folder she'll have divided things into 'urgent', 'read tonight', 'personal' and 'FYI'. There are around five or six things that will need to be dealt with every night.

7–7.30pm Every Monday I go to the pub and drink two large glasses of wine very quickly. The barman practically has them already poured as I walk in. I go with my sister and that's when we both get to say: 'Holy cow, what a week we have coming up.' I know it's not healthy and it's on a Monday, but it grounds me and helps me face, plan and get excited about the next few days.

7.45–8.30pm Home time, most nights. Before I've even got my jacket off, I help Harry with his homework and ask him how his day was. He's got a taste for the dramatic and will invariably begin, '*What* a day I've had!', so I've told him he has to tell me something positive before a negative. It's a whirlwind bath, bed and story-reading time.

8.30pm Supper. I'm lucky because Frank cooks and it's always a really lovely meal.

9pm By now I am beside-myself-tired but this is when I sit down with my red folder, scribbling on Victoria's notes so I can just hand it to her the next morning.

9.30–10pm Twice a week, including weekends, I'll be out for work or with friends, and will get home about now.

10–11pm I'm trying to get off my iPhone during this hour. But I can't help myself – I'll look at Facebook and Twitter, otherwise I feel as if I don't know what's happening in my friends' worlds. I'll sneak a look at one or two emails, look at my diary and text Victoria one last time before going to sleep.

'On Saturdays, I try not to do anything with work at all, not even looking at emails. All my electronic devices are set to silent when I'm in the house so that if I'm doing something with Harry we are not interrupted by any pings.

'On Sunday morning, Harry goes off to do sport and I'll go through my weekend folders. I have two: the usual red one and then a blue one, which is full of clips that I have sent Victoria all week for me to read. The red folder will also include any HR updates, KPIs, an indexed financial summary (I also get one daily), all of the reports to sign off and so on. I get it all done in the morning so that I feel as if I have the rest of the day to myself – if I have to do it in the evening, I feel like a schoolchild. Afterwards, I'll read through the Sunday papers and tear out plenty of press cuts – it's important that I'm on top of business news but also trends in our own concerns, what people are buying, what designs are interesting and so on. Then I pack my work bag and leave it by the door so there's nothing left behind and then I can catch up on *The X Factor*!

'What's good about my diary is that although I am relentlessly 'on', I am taking the temperature of the company daily because of my red folder system. People in the company know to send me an email marked 'Urgent' if it needs to be looked at that night.

'I take stock of absolutely everything in the company, from people, finance, creative ideas, press, new partners, new products ... My folder will include things such as what our reception is going to look like in the upcoming months (it's important to me – the first impression for our staff and visitors), our technical roadmaps, what staff we're hiring or firing. I need to know a little bit about everything and my team know to give me more information than I strictly need to have, just to satisfy that itch.'

SOPHIE'S HONESTY DIARY – THOUGHTS
ON AN AVERAGE DAY

'For me, there are two aspects of my work: the business of going to and being at work, which historically has taken place in the office; and my actual work, which happens at night, early in the morning, at weekends or on holidays. Even when working from home, the same principles apply. Daytime is communication, face time, collaboration. Personal productivity is an out-of-hours thing. So at about 6pm each day, as the office starts to thin out, I make a cup of tea and metaphorically rub my hands in relief and enthusiasm at the prospect of getting down to a couple of hours of proper work. Producing something – almost anything – is what I love to do and what I think I'm good at. Which isn't to say that meetings and chats with colleagues, travelling and workshops and so on aren't all highly valuable. Done right – with goals, structure and action points to take away – they're a great way to communicate, solve problems and work as a team. I'm not anti-meetings either, they're a great way to work together. (Although, seeing as we're being honest here, I could always do with a few less. My diary isn't pretty.)

'Ultimately my pressures come from deadlines, the chain reactions caused by plans and the endless mental and literal efforts to keep on top of timing. The biggest time stealers of all are the curve balls, whether big or small, which always throw you out because suddenly you have no time to deal with the stuff you had planned to do because the problem is going to take it all up.

'I've been lucky enough to have a truly brilliant PA, someone who can turn the resources of two people into at least three, if not ten. Someone who understands your needs and lays the path with everything you require in any given minute, hour or day amplifies your capacity beyond measure. Obviously, when we first began, I didn't have one and very recently, there have been a few months where I've gone without one (a bad PA is worse than no PA at all). Alone, I felt like a long-distance runner trying to maintain a Mo Farah-like pace, just to keep up with an intense diary of back-to-back meetings, deadlines and the inevitable crashing waves of thousands of daily emails.

'However, while I didn't get my cup of coffee brought to me just as I like it each morning, it meant I learned some valuable things about what I had to prioritise and get done in my day. For example, without the prop of being handed the correct paperwork before a meeting, I found myself better prepared. Having someone do it for you is not nearly as mentally effective as pulling together your own research/ reading/agenda. It also made me an all-round better-informed person because without someone filtering the specific work-related articles for me to read, I started noseying around all sorts of irrelevant and fascinating things, which of course threw up new ideas I might not have otherwise had.

'I made new and better connections at work because I was talking directly to more people instead of relying on someone else to do it for me. The most surprising discovery was that I generated and kept less paper. It's easier to find another way when you haven't got someone to file it for you. I even came bang up to date on twenty-first-century technology – travel planners, Google Maps, iPhone bother, the quirks of the office printer, useful apps and so on.'

So, that's us. We'd like you to do the same. As you can see, there are two approaches – a detailed breakdown and a broadbrush look at how your life is divided.

DAY 1 PRACTICAL EXERCISE:
WRITE YOUR OWN HONESTY DIARIES
allow: two hours

Do two versions if you can. One snapshot of a day that is fairly typical in your week, on an hour-by-hour basis. The best way to get a really honest view of this is to keep a detailed diary for a week; from that you should be able to see what happens most frequently and when. Then write down another diary that is more of an overview, thinking about how your life is divided up, helping you to find where the real work and play happen.

ANALYSIS

In many ways, our two diaries reflect our own approaches. Holly's every minute has to have a robust, tangible output; to be able to say, 'we achieved *this*.' She puts herself under massive pressure and of course that does translate to the rest of the team – they're put under pressure too. Sophie is different in that she needs output too, but will subscribe to results coming from the impetus and energy of 'just talking', sharing ideas and working out solutions, so long as everyone leaves the meeting clear and confident of what's next, which often she drills down to action points that she asks to see in a follow-up note afterwards. Investing time in relationships is time extremely well spent but it's the outcome that makes the difference. However, you have to wait for these results to come through and sometimes that time isn't available.

Our own roles and responsibilities as we grew notonthehighstreet.com continually changed, as we each found ourselves taking on different tasks. We were always happy to say 'I want to do this', even though we can admit many of those tasks were not planned and took some adjustment. Thankfully, because of the support we gave each other, we were able to be honest about what we wanted to try to do if we thought the end result could be fantastic.

Of course, it meant there were times when we had to be honest about when something wasn't working any more, and that was harder. We were joint MDs for many years and by keeping the conversation going we were able to be the honest voices in each other's head, always ready to have the discussions about what was going well and what wasn't, who would be best to fix something and so on. Keeping it simple meant these kinds of things were addressed quickly and easily, as part of our daily routine.

Eventually, as a result of these ongoing conversations, we were able to recognise the need for a more significant change in our roles – from joint MDs to CEO and Executive Director, later Director. That was back in 2011 and was based on us having an honest realisation that we would do the best by ourselves and notonthehighstreet.com if we divided up, with Holly leading the overall corporate, strategic and commercial vision as CEO and chairman of the board, while keeping a strong connection with all aspects of the business and with Sophie as Executive Director overseeing the business in a board capacity with focus on all things customer. This meant that Holly took up the helm in the core leadership role.

We were both doing our best work that way and reflecting our original partnership questionnaires – the ones we had filled out when we first became business partners, asking each other to be very honest about our expectations and vision for the company. It was only because we had been honest from the very beginning that as the business matured and its needs changed we were able to adapt and develop in a way that was not only possible but also comfortable and part of a natural evolution. We were able to enjoy what we did best and trust in each other too. This was reflected not just in our work within the company but also when we went out to do PR and interviews, with Sophie concentrating on consumer editorial and Holly on business and strategic interviews.

Finally, although it had evolved gradually over a couple of years, the biggest change of all was made in 2013 when Sophie came to realise that the time had come when her best work would be done for the company outside the office, stepping away from day-to-day management but remaining as Director, ambassador for the brand, a shareholder and sitting on the board. Doubtless, the two of us will continue to evolve our roles as the business keeps on growing as we plan for it.

DAY 2 PRACTICAL EXERCISE:
ASSESS YOUR WORKING DAY
allow: ten minutes at the end of three working days

At the end of each working day for three days in this period, ask yourself:

1/ What did I avoid doing and why?

2/ What did I most enjoy doing today and why?

3/ What do I wish I could have done today but didn't?

4/ What did I kick myself for and why? Was I unprepared or unskilled?

5/ What new thing did I learn today?

6/ What put me through my paces?

Given our changing roles, the way in which we analyse our working days now is, by definition, different. However, one thing we share: we believe that you need to know what sort of person you are in order to know how to make the most of your time at work.

We're all familiar with hearing how busy everyone is and we know we certainly feel that it is difficult to get everything done because of the shortness of time. But is that always the whole answer? Could it be that we use shortage of time as a way of avoiding the truth? 'I didn't have the time' is not, to be frank, the reason for not doing something. When it's a priority, or you have the ability, or you have the will to do it – you'll get it done. So when you said you didn't have the time, work out what you really meant when you said it. Did you truthfully mean that you didn't want to? Couldn't? Didn't have the skills? Preferred to do something else? This is the key to getting things done – finally. Or deciding never to do them because actually, they don't matter.

DAY 3 PRACTICAL EXERCISE:
YOUR (HONEST) LIFE IN COLOUR
allow: one hour

This exercise (and the one below) we learned from a business coach, Verity Lewis. It requires a look at the emotional, mental and physical commitments of your life. You'll then be thinking about whether you are happy with the picture that draws. For this exercise, we are thrilled to say that colour coding can be handy here (almost nothing we like more than visualising our lives through colour coding). Write down each thing that takes up your time – whether large or small, from VAT returns to cooking supper – and give it a rating of 1 to 3 that corresponds to how you feel about how productive or necessary that thing is. Put each – according to that rating – into columns headed 1. Must Do, 2. Should Do and 3. Shouldn't Do. You can use big and small stickers for big and small things.

Use colours that indicate whether you love or hate things – perhaps yellow for love it, blue for ambivalent, grey if it makes you miserable … you get the picture.

To make sure you've got everything covered, you might, for example, think of the different aspects that make up your current work (anything that contributes to your work life, whether it's in the office or related engagements), voluntary work (e.g. charity or parents' association), future career development (reading this book is a good start!), family (e.g. helping children with homework), home (domestics), personal goals (e.g. going to the gym) and social (e.g. catching up with friends).

Stick it all on to a huge piece of paper – we like A2 – and take a step back. If you've got lots of big stickers in your '3. Shouldn't Do' column, that's telling you not to waste your time. If everything's in grey, be kind to yourself, do more of what you enjoy – life shouldn't feel like a punishment.

So Holly, for example, has a chart with big focuses: there's a good chunk given over to future planning, thinking ahead for the business. And it's yellow. That's great, because she loves doing it, and it's important, so it's in column 1. But is it enough time, or should she make more for it? Or is it too much, when other areas are calling for her attention? She says below that she needs to get more of herself into the day-to-day business. Sophie's chart is fragmented, with lots of small amounts of time spent on lots of different things. That shows that she gets a huge amount covered, and is on top of all areas of her life, but she needs to work out what's part of the overall plan, in both life and career – and what's distracting her – then make those shifts to fully focus on just two or three key things that will make the biggest steps forward.

Let the chart talk to you ... it won't be hard to work out what you need to change.

We want you to achieve your long-term business plans and devise the goals that will help you make them happen. But before we look at goal-setting (which is the next chapter), it's vital that you look at yourself and the way in which you run your business. As our company has grown, we have had to evolve with it and sometimes we have had to face up to difficult truths about what we could and couldn't do, on two fronts – at work and at home. Those truths were hard to realise at first – 'What, you mean we can't do *everything*?' – but once we faced up to them and dealt with them, they were a fast route to professional freedom, allowing us to be even better leaders than before. That's what we want for you. So we're going to get personal now.

Holly: 'I'm always looking at ways of improving the business efficiency as well as myself – anything and everything. Which is as it should be – that's what builders do. In my latest review, I looked at how I could get more of "me" into the business. From my honesty diary you can see how long

I spend in meetings! One of the changes we are introducing, trying to lead by example in doing so, is that all meetings are now twenty minutes maximum and must have a clear agenda in place beforehand. External meetings must be no longer than one hour. I saw that I had to recognise the 80/20 rule of meetings – that if you do not have structure, then 80 per cent is wasted and only 20 per cent is useful or needed. Which means that we have a heck of a lot of people, and energy, including my own, who could be delivering better to the customers. I'm introducing this rule, will follow it and will be more and more out on the floor.'

PROFESSIONAL PERSONALITY PROFILING

Self-knowledge will help as a motivator, as long as it's supremely honest. For example, if you are a creative person and you get stuck in technical issues then you will feel very low, even if you've done a good job.

We've both done professional profiling and it's helped us a lot. There are many variants of this, but they all work to the same principles, which is to define your working style and personality into one of a number of set types. It gives your analyst, and therefore you and your colleagues (if you choose to share with them), a shorthand language and set of identifiers based on the most common human traits and variables that you can all understand, compare and develop. There are no wrong types. A series of questions – perhaps 200 – have to be answered quickly, honestly and without too much thought. Typically you might be identified as one of sixteen types. A follow-up psychoanalytical interpretation – ideally in person – will explain in much more detail what all this might mean to your work and career and why.

When the company was moving so fast, growing at such a pace and our own roles were constantly shapeshifting, it could be hard – at times impossible – to keep a handle on what we needed to do and how we were going to do it. The point about paying money for professional profiling is probably as much about the fact that it forces you to stop in your tracks and concentrate on the picture of your life. You need a professionally trained profiler to take you through the process and talk you through a detailed analysis afterwards. We can't recommend it more for your business and personal lives.

We do advise that you invest in this with a qualified practitioner (see The Directory) who will book a session and give you feedback. Doing a random quiz on the internet is not advisable. You might make big decisions based on something that has no substance. A proper feedback session will help you identify key development actions.

Ruth Cornish, HR consultant, carried out professional profiling on both of us. This, in summary, is what she had to say.

On Holly

'Holly's drivers are twofold: to prove the naysayers wrong and to build. For the builder, a point of satisfaction or saturation is never reached – there will always be a higher point to be aimed for. It's no coincidence that the business model is one that required everyone to think big from the start: notonthehighstreet.com gets better the bigger it is. Holly's great fear is of missing opportunities that might help her and her company achieve her goal. But she is also determined to keep going so that those who ever doubted her would know they are completely and utterly wrong.

'Holly's goals are best set by her. She will listen to others but she is firmly in charge. And she will change things but always upwards as she is a big thinker and has no sense of limits or boundaries. She is brave and has the courage of her convictions with a strong external energy that is infectious. This makes Holly both a natural and an exceptional leader because she energises and inspires everyone she meets. She leads others by sharing a vision they immediately feel excited about making happen.

'Holly's profile describes her as someone who is inspiring, imaginative, enthusiastic, charming, naturally curious and fascinated by relationships around her. She is energised by other people and has a strong intuition that has guided her when everyone has told her she was wrong.

'Because she is confident about her vision and is highly adaptive she embraces change with open arms. This means she is always looking for a new and better direction or focus for the business.'

On Sophie

'Sophie's driver is the desire to operate freely, to do what she believes is right and to take control of her life. The combination of not wanting to work unhappily for a company (as her father did), together with a deep discomfort with big, rigid institutions leads to the conclusion that she must own her own business. Also, Sophie is very motivated by the need for order – she likes a tidy desk, an immaculate house. To have order you must have control: control means you are self-sufficient. She will check and recheck any details or facts and will be the one that asks the questions others overlook. She wants to be sure of the substance of all her facts and likes to read into and understand things in great depth. She has very high standards. This means she is at her best when she is working for and hence relying on herself.

'She is also more of an introvert. An outgoing one for sure, but this means that she is as happy observing and working behind the scenes as she is fronting it all up. Sophie's goals, therefore, need to be step by step: things that she can see at once how to work through them and identify what is missing. She will always bring order to chaos because she is immediately calm and methodical and just puts her head down and gets on with it.

'Sophie is also highly motivated by relationships and how people are feeling. She will always consider the impact on her staff and colleagues of any decisions she takes. With her focus on the detail she is very clear in her communications with staff and what she expects of them. She is consistent, professional, organised, remembers things and follows them up. But she is also tuned in to how people are feeling and responds to that. She notices the small things and quickly understands how to play to the strengths of her team, understanding how to interact and engage with people to get the best out of them for the benefit of the business and all.'

DAY 4 PRACTICAL EXERCISE:
THE BREAKTHROUGH QUIZ
allow: three hours

This exercise, designed by Anton Teasdale, our acting chief people officer, is to help you discover exactly how you run your life and who you are. We're not saying it's easy and you need to pull your closest team around you to do it but it yields the fastest and most constructive results. Nor is this exercise just for you – it will help your team to find out about themselves and each other, which of course in turn will help you be a better leader. Anton has a reputation for an unusual and refreshing approach; if you can push yourself beyond your comfort zone you will feel the benefit fast. We're asking you to do something less ordinary here, but trust us on this one.

* Gather around you your top team or key players in your business. Everybody must commit to this process together – you will never forget this experience if you really go for it.

* The first stage is to open up to each other about your preferences, habits and rituals when it comes to what you want and what you need from others to be at your best. Ideally you should carry out this session just after you have had a real meeting so that you have fresh evidence. Everyone in the session should give and receive feedback on what it takes to get each of you to your best – it can be difficult to nail this so work through these questions and you'll gain the kind of insight you need:
  * How do you think? Do you reflect and mull? Or define a purpose then structure your thoughts towards an outcome? What happens if you try to approach things a different way? Can you adapt?
  * What are your routines and behaviour? Do you walk around to get your creativity flowing? Or get the flip chart out? Do you talk over people to be heard? Are you predictable or ever-changing?
  * What pleases you most when something goes right? Is it the

outcome itself, or the personal satisfaction for the team or yourself in getting there? What does this say about your skills?

Answer these questions as fully as you can with clear-sighted curiosity, and without judgement, to help you and the group explore what is driving the choices each of you makes.

✳ Using this, next explore what really lights your fire. A key component of leadership is inspiration. So you need to access and release your own inspiration. To do this, share the things – any things that you do, experience, have, want, see – that inspire you as openly and deeply as you can and do this, again, without judgement.

✳ Finally – take the leap. Reveal your personal turning points. There will have been three to five things that shaped who you are and made you the leader you are and the previous stages in this exercise will have begun to surface them for you to think more about now. You may not have recognised them as such before, but it won't take you long to see them now. Think back and try to recall defining times that made you take a certain path afterwards.

Revealing these moments means you will understand each other on a deeper level. All of you in the group will now be able to keep each other at your best, know what things to do and avoid, know why – and commit to it. It will be a privilege to be there. Enjoy it.

DAY 5 PRACTICAL EXERCISE:
KSI – KNOCKOUT SELF-INTRODUCTION
allow: one hour

This is a very American concept but one that is finding its way to the UK, so be prepared. Do you honestly know who you are, professionally, and what that means to your business network? Can you articulate it, clearly, truthfully and with impact? Because you absolutely must. As with your business, you personally need both a two-line and a ten-line elevator pitch ready to deliver straight off the cuff whenever you meet someone interested/interesting/helpful/useful on any kind of networking basis, or simply during a business meeting. You'd expect it to be obvious, but in fact it takes time to get this right, and it's worth it. It allows you to sell yourself effortlessly and naturally at every opportunity, to be always 'on' as far as your own personal pitch is concerned – and that's essential in business today. Your KSI will probably only really come together after you have completed some of the other exercises above, but it's good to get started on it even if it's a work-in-progress for a while.

Write down:

* **Name** (of course)
* **Education:** Just the highlights, this is your 'Ah, so she's a grammar school/self-educated/posh girl' headline moment.
* **Potted career summary:** Put this into types of work and really interesting achievements (rather than a chronological CV, which is

tedious) so 'I earned my stripes in media sales, then moved into management. I'm now head of XX at YY, running my own venture, which is Z.' Name companies if they're known and of course name your own if that's what you do.

✳ **A very little about your personal life:** '… and I live with my partner and two children in Richmond.' Needless to say, this is not the moment to air your relationship problems or say that you believe that reconciling with your father after fourteen years of estrangement is your single greatest achievement.

That information will give you the long version of your KSI – always take great care to tailor your response to the situation, question or meeting in hand, or you could come across way too strong! For the short version – which is really just an extension of a handshake on first meeting – edit it down to just your name, your current role and company, plus the most significant area of your work right now.

TAKING STOCK

While assessing the daily picture is a useful exercise it's also important to take stock now and then, making sure that you're on track for the bigger picture. We used to have an annual workshop – three days, just the two of us, going over everything we'd done in the past year and planning what was going to happen in the next twelve months, setting monthly goals. That's changed now – it's not just the two of us – because we have a senior management team, but there is still an annual meeting that takes stock in the same way. More immediately, there's a very structured week in our company, ensuring teams and colleagues meet, pushing along a very dynamic rhythm and cycle of discussion, agreeing goals, action points, reporting back on results, updating progress ...

We also had a board up in the office for a few years where all goals and milestones were posted according to deadline, and assigned an owner, so they got moved around the board every week – a bit like a battleships game. Every so often, as projects got completed and milestones hit, we had a session of adding new priorities to the board and so the cycle continued. This meant we had complete transparency throughout the company: everyone knows what everyone is doing and by when. It certainly focuses the mind!

THE TO-DO BOARD

If you don't already have one, put a big board up where you and anyone who works for you can see it. Pin up the goals and deadlines set for the company over the coming weeks and months. Make sure that each project is assigned an owner and keep the board up to date. It needs to be kept fresh or you will glaze over when you look at it.

Holly: 'There is a practical element to keeping the bigger picture front of mind, it's not just about visualising. You have to schedule planning for the future into your diary. I have my half a day working from home every fortnight or so and that time allows me to plan. On Monday evenings I can take stock of the week ahead. I need those times because the daily schedule takes up all my time. I'm not micromanaging because we're growing so quickly and I don't have an easily identified job, such as producing a catalogue with a nice project timeline and a deadline. I'm constantly pedalling. That's why it's so important to get off my bike now and then.'

FACING THE HARD STUFF

We like to think of ourselves as efficient: we can plan, we know how to get things done and there's almost nothing we love more than a big tick next to an assigned project. But there's a side to efficiency, where things get swept under the carpet. It might make everything look tidier but it means we haven't really dealt with the problem.

It's lonely being the boss, no question. We understand that and we'll acknowledge that it would be lovely if there were always someone at your side to give you a huge cuddle and say 'well done' after every difficult meeting or hard conversation. But the reality is that it is you and you alone who has to deal with the punishing elements of the business.

While you should know now that you need to face the hard things by being honest about what they are, breaking them down into smaller bite-sized tasks and dealing with them one by one, there will be times when life will throw you a curve ball and all your perfectly laid plans will go awry. Here are our survival strategies:

Take a deep breath

If you're feeling under pressure, the slightest thing to go wrong can send your stress levels through the roof. First things first: take a deep breath and ask yourself, is it really wrong? Or is it a problem? Or is it simply annoying? Could it even be a disaster that will get you – eventually – to where you want to be (as our software crisis at our launch put us on track to getting the right systems in place)? This last scenario will be harder to see when the initial fiasco happens but sometimes it helps just to know that that is a possible option.

Avoid complacency

The one thing we know about business is never to be complacent. If you think it's all going well, that's probably the moment you're about to get a very nasty shock. It's certainly happened to us in the early days of notonthehighstreet.com – the recession that struck not long after the business had really started to grow and the serious threat of a postal strike before Christmas (called off at the last minute) right after we had launched our catalogue, to name but two.

Planning for the unexpected is not always possible but you can plan how you would cope if circumstances beyond your control affect your business. The number one strategic response is: put the customer first. No matter what you are going through, are you looking after the customer above and beyond everything else? The point is that it's your relationship with your customer that makes or breaks your business; this is true at any time but it's particularly true during a bad time. Even when things go wrong and it's not your fault or your company's fault, your customers are unlikely to see it that way. Always talk to them as directly and openly as you can.

Dial 999 immediately

Emergencies must always be dealt with there and then. Never attempt a cover-up but communicate, communicate, communicate – to your customers and to your colleagues. Sometimes, without being ruthless or opportunistic, you may find that good comes from bad. A customer, colleague or staff member who feels that you are sincerely sorry may be more inclined to do further business with you. Everyone knows that bad stuff happens – the decision to be made is whom they would rather suffer a problem with.

DEVELOP THE HABIT

As the business gets bigger, the dice are more loaded and a little self-deception can end up being a big, expensive mistake. Now, if we fail to find the courage to say that we don't like, say, the creative idea for a TV ad (and being honest about creative work is extra difficult, because it's so hard to be objective) then it can mean the difference between hitting our financial targets or failing. Self-deception and avoiding the truth with others are habits like anything else. Don't slip into damaging ways. Get into the habit of being honest with yourself and others. Don't think of it as being mean – you'll have plenty enough emotional intelligence to deliver it with respect, good reason and integrity – think of it as treating time and money as the crucial things that they are in business.

Identifying your own strengths and weaknesses, and those of the team closest to you, will also help you be a better leader. You'll be a much clearer communicator; tasks will be assigned to those who can understand and complete them and confusion will no longer hold sway over your business.

WE ASKED OUR PARTNERS

What sorts of things crop up in your working day to make
you stuck or distracted? Do they tend to be the same kind of things
or is it always a surprise? Do you ever find these things result in an
overall outcome better than you could have imagined?

Pearl and Earl: Sometimes there are personal distractions such as children on their holidays. Or perhaps a current issue that needs firefighting – we always have to make time for issues with customers. Sometimes it is just self-induced, like getting lost on Pinterest or product research (the things I like to do) versus say accounting (which is not as much fun, but equally necessary). But the best unexpected things are opportunities that need to be seized! There are pleasant surprises. Sorting out a customer issue can mean you have uncovered an exceptional ally. For example an issue with some decorations led to discussions and resolutions for that order and then it turned out that the customer in question was a hotshot IP (intellectual property) lawyer who was so pleased that they offered some very helpful time for free. Last month we also had an email from a local friend saying that they had heard of some local grants being given out but the deadline for entrants was 5pm. We had our business plan already so I spent the afternoon adapting it and we found out on Christmas Eve we'd been awarded £20k.

Maria Allen: Some spontaneous ideas can result in really positive outcomes. For example: I read that our prime minister, David Cameron, had bet the New Zealand prime minister on a rugby match and he lost, so he had to wear a pair of kiwi bird cufflinks in the House of Commons. We make cufflinks so we made and sent him some. He then wore them in the House of Commons and tweeted a photo afterwards, which got us some great PR – TV, radio and coverage in national and local newspapers. So this was a great outcome from an initial idea that day and we have now created a new product from it too!

My 1st Years: Products going out of stock causes headaches. We may be selling a certain line extremely well and suddenly it goes out of stock and then we have to let the customers know that the product won't be back for a certain amount of time. We then have to work out what replacement product to offer and launch in its place until it arrives back in the warehouse. Also, staff calling in sick. This can be a problem as we need to arrange new staff in their place as day-to-day roles need to be filled. These are two examples of how a day can be distracted, resulting in a slightly less efficient day ahead.

Bookishly: I am very often distracted by emails and the internet in general. That is never a surprise and I have had to work hard at keeping on track. I like to answer customer enquiries immediately, and while that is a good thing, sometimes it isn't the most efficient thing to do. I *always* have about fifteen tabs open in my internet browser. On occasion I get distracted by a new product idea and end up researching and planning a pie-in-the-sky idea instead of focusing on what will make money immediately. That doesn't happen to me too often but new product ideas have sometimes taken off in a way that is better than imagined.

Where are you and your business going?

'Failing to set goals is like setting out on
a road trip without a map.'

MICHELLE MOORE

DAYS 6 TO 7

Identifying your thirty-day objectives as well as the
long-term goals for your business and yourself.

Now that you have a clear picture of what your working day involves, as
well as your overall vision of how your life is generally divided up, you will
start to think about what needs to change. These next two days are about
setting your goals to reflect this, in both the short and long term.

We know this can be tough to do but unless you set goals you won't have
a plan for how you're going to meet them. And having that plan will be
reassuring because at the very least, at the end of this chapter, you should
have some kind of a clue as to how you think you're going to get to your
end goal.

Sophie: 'When I first stopped being someone else's employee, after
I had Honor and left Publicis way back in 1999, practical goal-setting
became a vital part of the picture. Like almost every freelance writer I
know, especially those with children, I quickly realised that I couldn't just
take the work when it came – which would only ever be irregularly – earn
the fee and hope that the profit turned out right at the end of the year. At
first guess, I thought I'd need to do, say, an article a week. Not easy with
two small children but doable. Then I clearly remember doing the sums to
check that, dividing the annual income I needed to earn by the average
payment per article. That gave me my goal – and it was quite a shock: I

your goals

needed to write at least three articles a week. Which was going to nearly kill me – I'd be working night and day. I didn't even know if I could win that much business in the time, never mind deliver the goods. But I had to, we were really struggling for cash at the time and for a while I did find a way.'

Holly: 'Although Sophie and I have always written out goals for the business, I've never been able to keep to the discipline for personal targets. I had decided that it was about keeping the business on track and failed to grasp that my goals outside of the company's objectives were just as essential.

'2013 was the first year I set out to tackle things that I had left far too long. By the end of the year I had achieved them all, but more than that those goals set me free and made me a better leader, which in turn helped the business. It meant that year was by far the most progressive personally. I achieved all the goals and I don't mind saying it nearly killed me to get them all done in twelve months!

'Some of the goals for the following months were company related but things that mattered to me personally, such as developing the culture of the business or moving the offices. I also decided that it would be very important for me to receive coaching and that has been hugely, unexpectedly, beneficial. In doing so I removed negative energy and was very truthful with myself. I wanted to shape up and in doing so, I shaped up the business.'

Identifying your goals can be hard because you need to be audacious – enough to set a target when you are still at zero. You also have to overcome, or at least contain, the fear that you may not reach those targets. Failure, in short. This is harsh when the reaching of targets may be dependent upon factors that feel beyond your control, whether that's customers buying your products or a financier investing in you. But this chapter is about keeping your eye on the end goal – making sure you don't set your sights too low or sell yourself short – as well as working out what it's going to take to get there. Doing this will make you fearless.

We set ourselves targets from the beginning and now we think we're pretty good at knowing what we can achieve, making accurate guesses for sales figures and revenue forecasts. We frequently set what feel like impossible targets that we subsequently meet but we have underestimated ourselves occasionally, too – and then we are joyously surprised. In November 2012, we had a sudden and almost inexplicable surge in sales. For over a month, we beat our target every single day, sometimes by as much as 100 per cent.

At Christmas we have what we call our Santa tracker, a live online graph that is linked to our checkout, so everyone in the whole company can see how we're doing on an hourly basis. It's displayed as a staff-only web page on our internal data warehouse. It shows one line for the target sales figure, tracking across the screen from zero at 00.00 hours right up to the target figure at 23.59 each day. Then there's a second line for our actual results, in real time. If we're tracking below target, grumpy Christmas gremlins (some of our staff members, Photoshopped in costume), curse away in speech bubbles; if we're on or above target, various comely Santas (also Photoshopped pictures of staff) compliment us with speech bubbles of the very nicest praise. There are times when we get used to gremlins – hitting Christmas target is a rare thing as we aim so high – but this particular year, around late November, those jolly

Santas were full of festive glee as we beat our targets repeatedly and quite dramatically.

It was gratifying for all the usual reasons but also because we had taken a calculated risk, spending heavily on our marketing, which included a TV ad we were very proud of but which had cost us a fortune, and it was clearly paying off. It came at the end of a year in which we had missed quite a few targets, so we could hardly believe our eyes sometimes when our Santas gave us good news on top of great news, day after day. More than once we turned over double our target. That hadn't happened for years. It was a nice feeling and it felt like the start of something even bigger for the year to come.

Unfortunately, at the end of the year we closed short of our annual target. We had done well but not well enough. It's a good example of where even unexpected and outstanding success – that incredible Christmas surge – is only just enough, if it's even enough at all. While we should have been congratulating ourselves on making millions, the problem was that we had already geared up our spending to make target. We hadn't made the money, but we'd spent it as if we would: people had been employed, office space expanded, investors primed. Our 2013 projections were already written, based on meeting 2012 targets. Now they, too, were looking impossible. So it was a bittersweet ending to the year. We had to accept it as the consequence of being very ambitious and running an ambitious company.

The good news was that we had a whole new year in which to achieve the impossible and we were sufficiently uplifted by those amazing six weeks to believe we could do it. Sure enough, 2013 was a landmark year in so many ways: success built on success so that all those things – our team (of both senior and young fresh talent), our offices, our advertising campaigns – grew even bigger and better. Our brand was given a stunning new look and our site and product range improved and expanded to bring the 'life less ordinary' we knew our customers loved. Christmas 2013 saw us advertising not just on TV but on radio, the underground, national newspapers and magazines; it was the year we got big, with notonthehighstreet.com's name on everyone's lips. That simply wouldn't have been possible without those big audacious goals we set two years earlier.

THE COMPETITION

All along the way, it's essential to keep a close eye on what the competition is doing. Healthy rivalry has spurred many a business to success – encouraging entrepreneurs to set their goals higher, keeping creativity and imaginations edgy and maintaining a fast, furious pace. But keep it in perspective and focus on what makes your business unique.

Throughout the book, we'll ask you to consider the competition in the course of your practical exericses – make sure you do that.

THE BIG ONES: LONG-TERM GOALS

Everyone tackles goal-setting differently. Some can only think about the small, achievable targets, focusing on the first step that begins the thousand-mile journey people are so fond of talking about. Others can hardly tear their eyes away from the technicoloured big-screen picture. That was us.

We were bursting with barely contained euphoria about the big dream from day one of the business. The feeling that we were on to something that was not only very special but *achievable* – that we'd got there before anyone else – translated into a sky's-the-limit feeling. It meant that when we sat down to work out how we were going to achieve it and where the thousand-mile journey would lead us, it was a pretty stupendous place.

Broadly speaking, these bigger goals should be your overarching vision for the company. Perhaps you want a global online business that's bigger than Amazon – that's us! – or a bricks-and-mortar cafe of your own to sell your confectionery creations. There will be specific steps that need to be taken to reach these points, but as they may be part of a five- or even ten-year plan there will be a lot of unknown factors that need to be coped with along the way. Your task is to work out what those steps will be.

Reaching a big goal will almost always mean taking a pioneering approach. There will be no tried-and-tested road map, no pre-written to-do list to download, no instruction manual. The signposts that are your medium- and long-term goals are all things that you have to come up with. And it's difficult, which is why you need to keep your eye on the prize, clear as day, to keep you focused as you plan your strategy and the steps you'll take to get there.

When people talk about visualisation techniques – and we're all in favour of those – we sometimes found ourselves wondering why they're called 'exercises', as if they were something hard that you have to do. For us in the early days, the visualisation just kept on coming, unstoppably. We truly wish that for you too. It makes it all so much easier and so much more fun. Later, as reality sets in, it gets harder sometimes even for the biggest dreamer to visualise the outcome as a reality. We won't deny that we got weary, depressed and emotionally defeated at times. We were afraid we'd been fantasising, not visualising. But it's at those times that it's most important to keep that vision full of colour. It's what will help you get there.

DAY 6 PRACTICAL EXERCISE:
VISUALISATION
allow: fifteen to twenty minutes

Holly: 'I'm a really big believer in visualisation – it helps me for both my short- and long-term goals – and I practise it daily, usually on my walk to work.'

Find the space for thinking time in your day, whether it's your fifteen-minute shower in the morning, your commute to work or while you're chopping onions for supper. The longer you can spare, the better.

When you have your time carved out, make it a habit to go through your to-do list for the day ahead, or the following day, in your mind, thinking each thing through as to how you will complete each task. Don't spend a lot of time on it, as you will have already thought it through when you wrote your list. Just get yourself comfortable with the immediate tasks in hand.

Secondly, think about the rest of the month or year and visualise what will be happening at the end of that time period. This is to help you feel mentally prepared for what you will be doing then, so that when that time comes around it will feel both familiar and achievable.

Next, take two or three goals that have been planned for the year ahead, whether these are goals that have been set or events that are in your diary, and focus on them. Mentally work through each thing, planning every step. On each landing stage – that is, the medium-term objectives that are taking you to the final goal – imagine yourself telling someone else about it, explaining what's happening, how you got there and where you're going with it next. The purpose of this is that when it comes to actually discussing those things, you've already thought them out to the point where it will feel that you have done them already. This helps you feel in control, enables you to work out what can be done and what can't and gives you the confidence to go and talk about it with someone else in real life.

Finally, after you've finished the visualising, make a note of those landing stages as you'll need them for the exercise on Day 7.

Holly: 'In 2010, I scribbled down a bubble plan of the ultimate goals of the business, and stuck it on the front of an A3 folder, which contained all kinds of notes and tear-sheets. Recently, after having had countless visualisations for the company and feeling like a volcano about to erupt,

I pulled out the bubble plan and drew it up in full. Believe me, it was huge, with charitable foundations, high-street stores, property, global milestones and more – I felt that at least this task was done for the next ten years. It then gave me a clear understanding of what could be ticked off each year and what the business could handle and when. Now, I refer to this monthly.

'Once you've got your goals clearly defined – get them out. Make it big! I have a floor-to-ceiling white board from one end of the room to the other that has the main three goals for each quarter of the year. It has all the dreams and worries written up there. It means it doesn't go away and no one can miss it. Get things off paper on to the wall, even if you just paint a wall with blackboard paint and chalk it. Just don't let it sit in a file on the computer.'

SHORT-TERM GOALS

Short-term goals are the smaller tasks and deadlines that will tell you what you have to do – each day, each week or just once – in order to get the bigger job under way. This is what we call the day job. Managing these is what enables you to see the wood for the trees, while planning and visualising are what make the business thrive, grow and keep moving. Setting your practical action plan and giving yourself a time limit will keep you on track.

Sophie: 'Numbers and financial targets aren't the only goals but they're such clear ones. When Holly first suggested to me that we needed weekly, monthly and annual targets, my immediate response was to say "Yes! Of course!" as I too recognised the need. But I was also hesitant. I thought: "Really? But then we'll *know* when we don't meet them!" Besides which, there are the non-number goals and it's vital to give those equal prominence. Holly and I did a huge amount of collaborative list-making in the early days. In order to sell this much, we're going to have to do X, Y and Z tasks. That might have been – for Holly – "Sound out 100 new prospects"; for me – "Create a new piece of sales literature to use when the potential partners are approached." We'd each put our names against a task, take it away and it became a matter of honour to be able to come back and say, sharpish, "Done." Before long, the literature was produced, the new sellers were approached and brought onboard, the customers loved what they offered and there we were: checkout sales went up.'

GOAL-SETTING FEAR

Er . . . except when they didn't. And then you wish you hadn't set the goals at all. Not reaching the goal is *failure*, a dreaded word. So why set goals at all? Why not just work as hard as possible? Everyone knows the goal is to succeed and for the business to make a profit. Why does it matter exactly how much, when failing to hit the exact target could make everyone feel a failure? Setting targets can be massively demotivating if they are never reached. So why do it?

Because until you set goals you haven't asked how much more you can achieve and how far can you push yourself. As Robert Kennedy said: 'Only those who dare to fail greatly can ever achieve greatly.'

You might fail, yes. But you've got to take the risk. There's no point in setting an easy goal. It doesn't count – it's just saying what's going to happen. We know how miserable and frightening it feels to fail to reach targets – it's happened to us. We had a couple of years where we failed to hit targets month after month. It was partly down to the recession and partly because we were pushing ourselves incredibly hard, trying to touch a bar that was out of reach. But failing to reach our target didn't mean that we could step back and dial it down. Nope, as we said, by the time you've set the goal, you're already in it too deep. You've committed to costs – training, staff, technology, office space – that are essential to achieve the goal. Instead, when we didn't hit target we had to gear up more and spend more on those things, and on marketing too, which felt terrifying when we were already 'failing'.

How do you deal with it when failure happens? You can't always excuse yourself for the failure but you can, perhaps, congratulate yourself on the growth you have managed in a tough period and if you know that you have been working the hardest you possibly can then that's okay. Our early investors, Tom Teichman from SPARK Ventures and Mark Esiri from Venrex Investment Management, would remain encouraging and that was helpful. We would say to each other that we'd done well (and kind of mean it, but only for a second) but we'd also know: this is unacceptable. It *cannot* be this way. So we had to pick up and carry on, harder than ever.

We took lessons from it too. It can be harder to work out why you failed than why you succeeded (though that ain't easy either). And we picked over it forensically – we thought we had planned it all so carefully and yet we had been wrong. This led us to think that we needed better analysis and for better analysis you need better gear, which means more money to cover costs before you've even made a profit. In other words, all roads led to higher targets. So you see, there's no backing down.

Sophie: 'In those very early days, when we'd committed so much and reaching target was agonisingly slow, I was anxious for much of the time. Equally, I kept it in mind that if we ploughed on, calm and steady, we'd get there – we had planned how to get there, we just had to stay on course. Still, for many months, I couldn't sleep at night. My heart would be racing far too fast and my imagination would run away with me about what might go wrong if I didn't do something right, *right now.* Once or twice, I went downstairs in the depths of night, made a cup of tea and worked out what it would cost for us to shut down and walk away with our heads held high. What bank loans we would have to repay, what last pay cheques would have to be written for the people who had worked with us so loyally and I calculated the total of the many bills already due for rent, marketing, technology. That could be a pretty scary number, even in the earliest months. I knew there was no way we could cover it personally. That was letting myself go to the darkest place, so that then I could deal with it, emotionally.

'Somehow, after that, it was easier. I'd worked out what we'd have to turn over in order to cover that ultimate cost. And how long that would take, at the rate we were going. In other words, I had in my head a figure for the magic moment of success that would put us in the clear. That was thanks to the revenue forecasts that Robert, Holly's father and our then finance director, was endlessly preparing for us. Then it was just a matter of time. So long as we battled on we *would* reach the place where revenue targets and planned costs cancelled each other out – we'd break even. I think that's how in the end I was ultimately fearless, because however bad it got, I had these ways to check back in and know it was possible.'

QUALITY QUOTAS

Reaching for your target is sometimes as important as actually hitting it. In fact, we'd recommend that you don't always strive blindly to achieve a set goal before allowing yourself to move on to the next thing. We believe in 'quality quotas', which means the point at which you have balanced a drive for excellence with the reality of simply getting a task done. Sometimes, you will have to make your peace with imperfection. We don't mean settling for second best but allowing yourself to see that you've got something as near to perfect as you can for the time being. Too many people put off launching a business or project because they haven't got their ducks in a perfectly straight row. Sometimes, 'good enough' really is just that. You can always reframe the end goal – calling it a 'soft launch', for example, which means you're still dealing with teething problems. We would never send anything out that we knew was substandard but we're also careful not to be perfectionists.

Holly: 'I've always been comfortable with goal-setting. It's a language I know and my training in advertising sales helped me get to grips with the metrics involved. Right from the start, I aimed for all 'As' in my exams because I knew even then that by reaching for what seems to be impossible you often achieve it. And even if you don't quite make it – as I didn't with that particular goal – you end up falling on the stars rather than the moon. A 'B' grade may not be an 'A' but it is still much better than a fail. Frankly, I relish a target, however scary. It's what makes me tick.'

When we started pitching to new businesses, it was as if we were putting on an ice hockey league tournament. There were scoreboards, bells ringing and team huddles. But it meant that we could all see how, if a massive, apparently wildly ambitious numerical target was set, then broken down into lots of little related metrics, it would then become achievable. So long as you went at it harder than you could imagine. Drawing up these goals on to the wall and saying them out loud made failure impossible: we *had* to do it.

SPECIFICS AND ACCURACY MATTER

While the setting of certain targets can feel as if you are sticking a finger in the wind, accuracy matters. Apart from anything else, it helps you in a practical sense because everything gets broken down into smaller, specified targets in order to help you build the bigger picture.

Let's take a couple of examples relevant to us at notonthehighstreet.com. The big goal: a new piece of customer-facing technology on the site. This breaks down into smaller goals: revenue targets, operations, deadlines.

Or, the big goal: rebranding. Broken down into smaller goals: customer insight, partner support, design, site functionality, site navigation, product inventory, messaging, marketing, financials. Each of these, of course, breaks down further into bite-sized tasks.

To justify spending time and money on work towards reaching an objective, you have to attach a revenue figure to it. (First and foremost, your business has to earn money. That means costing every minute you spend on it, ensuring a true, measurable profit.) Revenue forecasting is not something only an algebraic genius can come up with but you do need to dedicate some headspace to it. Start with what you're currently earning/selling/grossing, then add numbers that are, at this stage, no more than educated guesses about what your new objective or launch might earn. What training might you need? Might you need to absorb some losses or a cut in revenue in order to take a big leap forward? How many more customers might you bring each day? How much more might they spend when they do come? How much sooner might they come back when they know you do this/offer this new product/ service? Be bold and commit to the numbers that those guesses suggest. Once that is done, it becomes part of the workflow and you can begin to see deadlines, briefs, projects that will need to happen in order to get there ... those are the specifics and the details that get the job done. And always know this: long-term goals will change and all your sub-goals and objectives will have to be attached every time. That's the merry-go-round that keeps it all alive.

DAY 7 PRACTICAL EXERCISE:
SET YOUR THIRTY-DAY OBJECTIVES
allow: two hours

Take your notes from the Day 6 Visualisation exercise, in which you wrote down the landing stages you need to hit in order to reach your long-term goals. It's these that we want this book to help you arrive at in the next thirty days. We'll bet that most of your landing stages depend on addressing areas that we've had to face into at some point – money, reaching your customer, managing your team, sorting out your home life, as well as the tools and skills you'll need to do that, from confidence to time management. That's what this book is structured to tackle.

This next bit requires a little bold thinking but it will give you the boost and direction needed to walk through the critical steps towards your end goal.

Take a big piece of paper or start a new spreadsheet and do this:

1/ Create a table with space for headers across the top and down the left-hand side (lightly mark out a grid if you're not doing this on a computer).

2/ Across the top, write down the landing stages you have already identified. These should be practical objectives that will improve your career or your business, whether that's winning a major pitch, designing a new product, mastering new technology or turning something loss-making to profit. Use the things you visualised and write them down. Keep it to a few – maybe even only one or two.

3/ Down the left-hand side, list the areas we are going to cover in the coming weeks: team, confidence, money, sales, home life.

4/ Now, make a note where your landing stage and areas that you need to address meet on your chart. If, for example, winning a major pitch means addressing issues with your team, understanding your customer better and being more confident, put big Xs at the appropriate intersecting points. As you read the relevant chapters and do the exercises, bear your goal in mind. If you can – here's your sub-goal techniques coming into play – spend some time thinking specifically what it is you, say, need to address with your team, and make a note of that, too. Remember that being specific is what gets you to your goals, so invest time in getting clear – and being honest with yourself – about what it is you need to tackle. Don't worry if it seems difficult or horrible – that's what we're here for.

5/ Do the same with your other objectives, if you're tackling more than one, noting what it is in particular you need to focus on as you read through the book and work through the exercises – as well as learning from our experiences – in order to make that goal a reality in thirty days' time.

MEASURE, MEASURE, MEASURE

'Measure, measure, measure' is close to being the company mantra: we repeat it frequently to each other and to our staff. Any business start-up will review how it's doing at three, six and twelve months but even once you've been up and running for a while, you need to keep up the measured pace.

And if you measure, you must also record, record, record. Keep a note of your results so you can see patterns emerging and clues as to what works.

Recording how your career or business is faring is what will give you the ongoing clarity of vision necessary to ensure that you carry out your plans effectively. When we have pushed ourselves, with our senior managers, to agree on our future plans we then look at what steps we need to take to achieve them. We'll also agree there and then as to how we'll keep a record of achievements and learning as we go. We ask ourselves: what defines success here? It's not always obvious, so be sure there's agreement between you and your business partner or the colleague working most closely with you on the task. When you've measured and recorded, communicate those details to your wider team, if you have one. Share the results as well as the objectives and you will get everyone motivated to reach the same goal.

One other thing: monitoring your results – whether it's email enquiries that were converted into sales or which web pages on your site are generating the most traffic – is made a lot easier with digital and online tools such as Google Analytics.

KEY PERFORMANCE INDICATORS

Key performance indicators (KPIs), a well-used business term, is the catch-all phrase for those measurements of your company that demonstrate its health, or otherwise. If you own your own business, you should know your KPIs like the back of your hand. Tracking them regularly builds a picture that means that you will learn what to expect, so you'll spot anything going wrong and can deal with it quickly. At the same time, you'll also see where your strengths lie and therefore where to focus your energies and what to do more of.

KPIs can, however, easily feel rather jargony or too general, as with 'sales' or 'traffic'. Our three tips to make them rather more engaging are:

1/ Identify the precise nature of the KPI that's relevant and specific (for instance, we talk about TTV – total transaction value – rather than sales, to avoid confusion with our other sales channels).

2/ Write a description about what each KPI actually means – otherwise people can easily misinterpret your intention. Make it clear and human.

3/ Use motivating language when describing or naming. A company we knew called the group of returning customers 'You can't keep me away'. Well-named and described KPIs will get more acknowledgement, higher recognition, greater ownership and cause far less confusion. Be creative.

Create a KPI spreadsheet and, once you've decided what to track, record everything, always, so long as you're in business. There's software that can do it for you, of course, but only you can actually look at the numbers and think about what they're telling you. It's exactly the same as looking at your personal bank account and knowing that the overdraft means there's no pretending you didn't get carried away at Christmas.

Typically, your spreadsheet should include these minimum daily/ weekly/monthly numbers for:

✳ Number of enquiries/leads/traffic interactions (how much interest you are generating).

* Number of transactions.
* Your conversion rates (what percentage of your leads turn into sales).
* Sales in £s.
* Average price spend per transaction.
* Number of new customers.
* Number of repeat customers.
* Comparisons for all of the above to last year/month/week or all three.

You will undoubtedly add many, many more KPIs to these core ones over the months and years – you may well be able to identify some of them already – but these are a good place to start. We now have hundreds of pieces of data we watch regularly throughout the business and we've gone into more detail about these in The Back Pages.

LOOKING AHEAD

Setting goals and planning how you're going to reach them is crucial to the success of any career or business. Be audacious! Have a big dream and hold on to it – use visualisation daily to remind yourself of where you're going. Find your pioneering spirit and harness it to take you on the ride to that pot at the end of the rainbow.

At the same time – never let go of the specifics. You need to detail the steps that will help you climb that ladder of success. We know it's hard – sometimes your foot will slip and you'll have failed at that particular task. But you've got to take the risk – without it, you'll never know how far you can truly go.

Treat every step as a costed investment. Setting a target means commitment – both to the things you'll say you'll get done in order to hit it, as well as to the costs of training, equipment or staff you may need. All objectives must be measurable – and they must be recorded.

And remember to praise yourself! Always find a moment to take a step back and think about what you've achieved and why. We know you *can* do it – so long as you know exactly what it is you want to do. Good luck.

WE ASKED OUR PARTNERS

Do you set goals and objectives? If yes: what have
been the most audacious? Did they happen?
If no: do you think you should?

My 1st Years: My business partner and I set the goals and objectives for the year and for each month as well. Our most audacious was to triple the business growth each year. It has happened, yes.

Becky Broome: Goals and objectives help a business to better itself and encourage growth. Yearly, monthly, weekly and even daily goals are important. Even if they aren't always fulfilled it is good to have a plan and for the whole team to know what the goals are so you can work together to move the business in the same direction.

Oakdene: I set myself multiple goals for different areas of the business, some of them are very much numbers based, while others are more for personal motivation. A couple of years ago I had the personal goal of buying a sports car at the age of twenty-two; that was quite an audacious goal that I was just about able to achieve!

Ellie Ellie: Yes, constantly. If you don't write it down it doesn't exist! Writing down goals and objectives means they are real and they are going to happen. We always think and act like our goals have already happened in order to manifest ideas and focus even our subconscious on our goals. We even write letters to ourselves in the future, telling our future selves what we have achieved.

Running a business is full of bold risks but along with those come excitement, adrenaline and thrills! Since starting the business the most audacious objective was to start employing staff. It was a big risk moving from being self-employed at home to having an office with staff. I always focus on the bigger picture and how the business can benefit in the long run.

Sophia Victoria Joy: Absolutely, this has been crucial to the success I have so far enjoyed. My goals are constantly changing and stretching. As soon as a goal looks achievable in any way I will stretch it further and always push harder. Every goal seems audacious. I have never set myself a goal that wasn't! But so far I have achieved every goal I set, so although they begin by appearing audacious, they are in fact achievable.

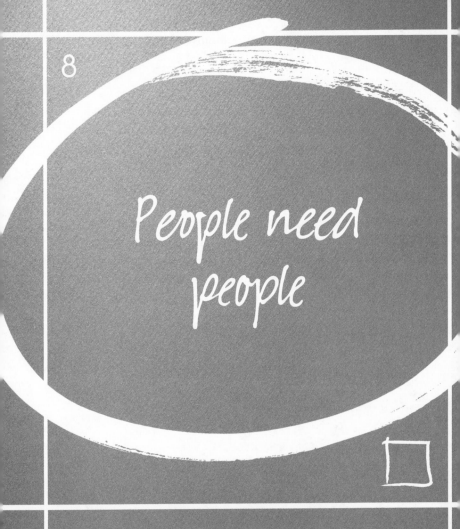

8

People need people

'In most cases being a good boss means hiring talented
people and then getting out of their way.'

TINA FEY

DAYS 8 TO 10

Getting clear about what you expect of yourself, your colleagues
and employees and what they are entitled to expect from you;
knowing how to motivate yourself and others; how to hire and let go.

This chapter should be a compelling one to take on board because as you
begin to hire more experienced staff and work with investors they will
often – indeed it is great that they do – have more management experience
than you. This brings expectations from them about how they want to be
managed and a need for you to ensure you are not managed by them. This
chapter will mean you are properly briefed and will know what needs to be
done and how.

When we first started notonthehighstreet.com we were, of course, already
grown-ups, with between us two marriages and a divorce, three children,
extensive experience in advertising, sales and publishing, a book and all
the usual crises that being an adult involves. We'd led teams, staged big
launches, managed senior clients and won major pitches. Yet we look back
on ourselves eight years ago as *babies*. We compare ourselves now with the
women we were in those early days of building the company and can only
marvel at how green we were, how naive, how innocent!

In some ways, this shouldn't be so surprising. Starting a business can take
you back to zero and as it grows so you evolve with it. That in itself can
change how you relate to others.

manage your team

The marker for us was when we realised that people who worked with us no longer saw us as two women working our own way through but as the bosses. We were expected to provide direction and focus, to know what we were doing. We knew that we had to inspire our employees, motivate them to work hard and keep up morale no matter what we knew was going on behind closed doors. It changes things, of course it does. Is it okay to cry at work when there's two of you? Yes. When there's ten of you? Not so much.

We've always known that the people in our company are its greatest asset. That's true of any business. We have limitless passion and vision, but we know we cannot – and do not want to – do it alone. Together with our people, we can bring all the skills, time and commitment (as well as sharing the enjoyment and the desire for a life less ordinary) that our business is built upon. Leading our team was relatively simple when we started, for the bare fact that there were very few of us. That's changed. Where we used to sit down for a chat, now we have senior leadership meetings. Where we used to dig in and get things done by spending the weekend in the office, now we have to brief teams, set a deadline and go away because there's nothing we personally can, or should, be doing. It's their job, not ours and it would be bad leadership to do it ourselves. We have true experts in the company, people who know far more than us. People we can ask what to do, what is right, what is normal – and they are people who are working with us all the time. We're not constantly hunting down someone's expertise any more.

Not that they always get it right, either. We're dealing less with the practical to-do list as leaders and more with personalities, careers and, yes, even politics. Sometimes, it's less about learning to live with our own mistakes and more about learning to live with other people's – embracing and learning from them as much as we ever did with our own.

Oddest of all, people come to work for us and we don't know who they are. We don't conduct every job interview; we have to leave the majority of that to our senior managers. We work hard at knowing names and saying hello, and we're always looking for people who are making a difference, doing outstanding things – but equally, we have to trust in our management structure that great people are not getting lost or wasted.

Our partnership and the way in which we work for the company have changed too; we had to face that because it all got so big, we couldn't possibly stay on top of all of it and we had to draw the line. That meant that at one stage, we formally divided things up: Holly took finance, merchandise, partners and HR; Sophie took marketing, customer service, copy and brand; design sat in the middle between us. We had weekly one-to-ones with each of our heads of departments, so that between us we knew what every department was doing. We would talk to each other a lot, but equally we knew not to bother each other if we didn't have to. That lasted until 2010 when we hired our COO (chief operations officer, a role that typically covers supply lines, logistics, customer service, infrastructure, premises and so on). Once he was embedded at notonthehighstreet.com and we had a strong marketing team, our roles shapeshifted again until we no longer ran any departments but were the co-founders and leaders of the business in each of our different roles.

What we're talking about is, of course, human resources. HR broadly divides into two – equally vital – areas: administration (payroll, holiday forms, sick pay and contracts) and development (opportunities, challenges, insight and leadership). We have made the mistake in the past of concentrating on one at the cost of the other but we have come to realise that both sides of the coin matter. One is useless without the other.

As an employer you need to be reliable and administratively sound but you also need to excite people, engage them, grow their careers and make them feel they're achieving something. Don't scrimp on this and you'll build a team who will go to hell – then heaven – and back with you if you ask them to.

With that in mind, think of this chapter as an audit of *all* your people skills and resources. Be your own Mary Poppins for the next few days, to make sure that you're doing all the right things, that you have the right skills within your team (and in you) and that your HR admin and operations are tip-top. Swallow down a nasty dose of medicine if you have to but face up to what needs to be done, even the backbreaking heavy lifting or, worse, heartbreaking decisions, and everything else will run more smoothly as a result.

PART ONE: ADMINISTRATION

This is what we and HR consultant, Ruth Cornish, call 'the trains running on time', the operations that make up the detail of employing someone. It can be tedious and it involves a lot of legwork but you must do it right – this is how you treat your employees with respect, earning theirs and building trust. Don't leave them wondering what's happening or where they stand. Their livelihoods depend on those forms, contracts and payslips. Deal with these foundations first and we can move on to the fun stuff later on in the chapter.

Operations include:

* Recruitment and hiring.

* Employee contracts, terms and conditions, legal compliance, working conditions, health and safety.

* Pay and benefits, the payroll and managing the administration of it all.

* Staff handbooks, HR policies and procedures.

* Employee relations – usually when things get tricky and things come to an end. It might be a staff member who is simply not engaged in the way that you hoped and is failing to deliver or develop, but it might be that they are recurrently ill or bring personal issues to work every day. It may be resolved mutually; it may be when you let someone go.

DAY 8 PRACTICAL EXERCISE: GET YOUR HR HOUSE IN ORDER
allow: one day

This audit is designed to help you identify any gaps or problems that need addressing. Plan when to do this and consider doing it at the weekend when you can work in confidence and without interruption. Remember you have legal obligations to keep any personal data on your employees confidential so if someone is helping, ensure they understand this and can be trusted. A simple nondisclosure agreement or confidentiality statement is the best way to do this – standard form documents are available online.

We recommend you get someone suitably qualified to check any employment documentation and make sure it is legally compliant, together with consulting on any issues that are unclear or that worry you as a result of your audit. Independent HR or legal professionals can do this.

Complete these tasks no matter how arduous – the long-term benefits are invaluable.

See The Back Pages for the HR audit to complete.

LEGAL OBLIGATIONS AND CONSIDERATIONS

Make sure you're clear on your obligations as an employer, especially around insurance, health and safety, contracts and letters of employment, disciplinary procedures and terminating employment contracts, PAYE, NI and declaring income, and paid holiday. Every staff member with more than two months' service should have a written statement of their terms and conditions, aka an employment contract. The government provides an online service that offers information and resources for employing people, including payroll, holiday, time off for other reasons such as sickness, maternity/paternity, health and safety in the workplace, template employment contracts, and policies and procedures. A good independent HR provider will be able to help too, but as your business needs will change very quickly avoid signing up to long-term commitments.

See The Directory for government guidance, regulations and HR resources mentioned throughout this chapter.

HIRING

It all begins with the hiring process, which starts long before you advertise the role or start interviewing. Your long-term staffing strategy depends on a complete cycle of good experiences, both in and out of the business. An employee's experience begins with the company's reputation: what are they hearing about you out there? Have they already half-wondered if yours would be a great company to work for? Some of our best staff initially approached us purely because they'd seen and heard about us, not because they'd been invited to by a job ad. They know, because we're a public brand, that we're about quality, originality and out-of-the-ordinary ways of doing things, so they can make a pretty safe assumption that working for us will embrace all those things. But more than that, we know there must be no image-reality gap when people step inside, so we're careful, for the good of our employees and our future hires, to create a workplace that is fun, rewarding, exceptional, fair. Only by doing that can our reputation go before us, as well as sustaining the commitment and delivering on the promise it implies to all of our staff. So from ensuring that we have a charming, less-ordinary workplace, to treating all candidates, hired or otherwise, with total respect and considering our staff's own careers, enjoyment and satisfaction, we invest much thought and care into making the entire experience of working with us a positive one.

Here's what we suggest:

✳ Before you even think about drafting your job spec or placing a recruitment ad, work out how your culture and reputation fit in and how it can be expressed well. When we hire, as well as the role itself (which is central, of course) we can talk about our purpose with small businesses and customers alike, and also about the fun stuff that's consistent with what people expect from our brand: our regular bake-offs, popcorn Fridays, the Golden Cupcake Award for our employee of the month, our ALM (Annual Love-in Meeting) and of course lots of out-of-the-ordinary parties.

✳ Present yourself and your company to the highest standards at every single touchpoint, from the advertisement to correspondence to the cup you serve tea in. The onus is on you, the employer, just as much as it is on the candidate to show that you are professional, polished and exceptional.

✳ Consider carefully where you might find your perfect candidate and think laterally. You may be just as likely to discover them through contacts in unrelated sectors, the school playground or at your yoga class as you are by advertising in your trade magazine.

✴ Look after your candidates and show that you value them, from their initial call or application to your first response, right through the process. Even those you decline. *Especially* those you decline. Follow up after each stage, keep them informed. Funnily enough, almost the same principles apply for the candidate and the employer. And in this multi-media age, any candidate is also a prospective customer and vice versa.

✴ Prepare fully and thoroughly for the interview and be prepared for them to interview you back. If they are good – and you want them to be – they should be doing all the same checks as you are, with charm and professionalism.

✴ Be sure they fit your culture and share your values. That doesn't mean they have to be the same as you or someone you'd invite to dinner every weekend. But can you see them belonging, finding their place, being halfway there before you've even begun to explain what you feel or mean about something? We test this rigorously through our values acronym: I AM REAL. In every interview we seek out evidence that the candidate is: Instinctive, Ambitious, Meaningful, Real, Exceptional, Analytical and Loving. These qualities can present themselves in lots of ways – we're looking for variety, not carbon copies – but being able to check off those qualities gives the reassurance we need.

✴ Be sure they can do the job. Are they qualified? Have they done this or something similar? This is a no-brainer. Don't be tempted to bypass this one because you've fallen in love with a candidate or become desperate to fill the post. See The Back Pages for a guide to interview questions.

* Explain very thoroughly – use a written job description too – the role, the brief, the commitment you're looking for. Is the balance of desire right? Do they want the job as much as you want them?

* Think about the future. Can they grow in the business? What's their long-term potential? Hiring for now is fine, but make it clear, or a fixed-term role. Permanent roles need a future or it gets very difficult for both sides.

* Share the decision-making – involve someone you trust, ideally an experienced hirer. Share all your feedback in a balanced, considered way. Keep notes on each candidate then consider each candidate and each criterion in turn. Gut instinct and your emotional reaction should be one of those criteria, so listen to that. Just don't forget the other criteria too.

THREE GREAT HIRES: WHAT THEY DID FOR US

While working to all those rules, there's always a magic moment when you know you've struck gold. We rarely fall for gimmicks or elaborate gestures, just hard evidence that this is what we've been looking for. These are just three of ours:

* The department head who came to be interviewed at a moment's notice, on a Sunday, at a wedding fair, just a year or so into the business. She told us everything we needed to hear in the only time we had – a flat fifteen minutes – describing the role, our values and her enthusiasm. We hired her on the spot.
* The technical lead who presented part of his application in the form of one of our web pages, demonstrating not just technical

skills but the wit, creativity, attention to detail and ability to connect with people that we were looking for.

* The design and copy manager who picked up a competitor's mailshot that was lying on the table during her interview, instantly spotted a proofing error, recoiled and said, 'There's simply no excuse for it!' We knew then that we'd found that shipshape approach, mixed with lots of warmth, that we wanted.

POLICIES AND PROCEDURES

You should have some simple written policies and procedures in place to meet your obligations as an employer and to protect your business. Key ones are sickness absence (what to do when someone is off sick), disciplinary (include in this policy examples of gross misconduct), grievance, and health and safety (to be guided by the Health and Safety Executive, which provides a helpline and an excellent employers' pack for £35).

You may want to add to this as you grow and issues come up. You need to review any documentation that you have in place on an annual basis. Try to write things in a way that will help staff understand what you expect of them and the consequences – positive and negative. Get some professional guidance to ensure that they are legal and serve their purpose. In the event of any dispute it will come down to how clear you were in the first place.

LETTING PEOPLE GO

Making the decision to let someone go is as important as hiring. Just as you need to think carefully about employing someone for the business, you need to keep a close eye on whether your employees are successfully working on your behalf.

Naturally, some people will leave entirely of their own accord sooner or later – that's the normal cycle of things. (A few may stay forever, until retirement ... You must, of course, do all you can to keep the good ones as long as possible.) Only occasionally does one intervene and even then, it should be because it's in order to do right by all. Very occasionally you have to terminate someone's employment contract purely because they misled you or failed you badly, but these circumstances are rare. But perhaps because the common cases are rarely talked about, there's not much in the way of guidance around and it's ultra important to get the process as right and fair as possible.

If you believe you have reason to end someone's employment, try not to be afraid of the process. It's likely that if it's not working for you, it's not working for them either, so ultimately it's good for all sides that you address the problem – though we readily admit it can be some time before everyone agrees on that. It's not pleasant but stick to the procedure – call the employer advice line at Acas, who can talk you through this – and you can make it as painless as possible for both sides. Getting it wrong can be expensive, not just in terms of the costs if it goes to court in an employment tribunal, but the impact on you and your business. Especially you. So be sure to get good advice that you trust – that can be an HR specialist, who might be more pragmatic than a lawyer and could be right for your situation.

Holly: 'From our experience, the moment you decide "That is it, they *have* to go" you are probably at least six months too late. This should make you feel better as now you know you are right. It has taken us as long as a year in the past to realise someone was no longer right for the business; with experience, we've been able to recognise the signs more quickly. We trust our gut instinct better now. The more unpractised or scared you are, the longer you will bury your head in the sand.

'It's easier to address these situations in cases where a person has been destructive. You wouldn't, for example, stand for it if someone was bullying your child or breaking into your house – so why stand for it in business? Having a framework, planning for the aftermath well in advance and keeping it unemotional really helps.

'The idea of having to part ways with a long-standing employee is naturally very upsetting. But for the health of the business, sometimes you have to realise an important principle: if you can't change the people, change the people.'

(YES THERE ARE) HAPPY EMPLOYMENT ENDINGS

There are times when ending an employment relationship is the only right thing to do. Handled expertly, this can bring a successful – even happy – outcome for both sides, even where there is great loyalty and a long-standing partnership. We've seen this at first hand and heard of many other founders learning the same thing. Ruth told us about a case where she was brought in to troubleshoot a company's failing operations. It was immediately clear to her that the trouble lay not with the company, but with a loyal and hardworking senior partner of twenty years, Amy, who was not qualified for her role and was unwittingly blocking the company's progress, recently widowed and deeply unhappy. The owners' primary concern was to avoid confrontation and upset with Amy, so letting her go was – they believed – out of the question. Not only they, but also Amy and the company itself, were tied up in knots. Yet as soon as Ruth was able to work out what Amy really wanted to do with her life, she was able to make her an offer that was generous and fair, saw her weeping with relief, retraining and starting out in a new and fulfilling business of her own. Amy retained a warm and close relationship with the business, attending parties and events for many years, during which time she even remarried. Ruth heard the owner recently telling the story to a manager, saying how important it was to make such decisions so everyone could move on.

TEN GOLDEN RULES OF ENDING EMPLOYMENT

1/ Know why you are doing it. Be very clear. Be impartial. Be fair. Be balanced and proportionate in assessing the situation and what you plan to do about it. Think through the process in detail, plan it, manage it and lead it.

2/ Always get independent advice. Take advice not only on what they have done but what you can do about it; you may be able to do more than you think. Acas has a free, pragmatic helpline for employers.

3/ Always follow your internal procedure. These are your policies on disciplinary, sickness absence, capability, redundancy, probation and so on. If you don't have a policy on any area, be guided by Acas. No matter how fair or appropriate your decision is, don't open yourself to tribunal proceedings by failing to follow your own procedure.

4/ Remember the three Rs: records, records, records. Keep a detailed file, recording everything in writing, listing attendees of meetings, time, date, who said what. File everything even if simply by writing notes in an email to yourself.

5/ Only say what you are willing to repeat in public. Everything in emails or texts could be disclosed later, so avoid saying anything that could lead to difficulties. Equally, don't panic if something slips out. Address it, retract it, move on.

6/ Christmas is not a good time for dismissing people. Avoid it if you can, along with the bad press you will get externally and the low morale internally. Likewise, don't do it on a Friday when it's too late for the employee to make any calls or plans about getting a new job and all they can do is worry until Monday.

7/ Be as generous as you can. Even just by letting them keep the laptop that bit longer. Employees that have been treated well, respected and allowed a dignified exit are much more likely to move on quickly.

8/ Do not confuse redundancy with dismissal: positions can be made redundant but not people, so if you make someone redundant you cannot replace them with someone else in the same position. Saying someone is redundant but writing a letter citing a performance issue as the cause is likely to make this unfair dismissal.

9/ Never get personal. If you feel that you are too personally involved, get someone else to lead the meeting. When emotions are running high, things can go too far off course.

10/ Once you've made your decision, move swiftly and decisively. Follow the correct consultation periods and procedures, but no more. It can make things harder.

Holly: 'When we moved the company to our third offices at Lion House, it signified a moment where we all had to grow up and it meant making changes to our senior team. But it's a natural thing and you have to deal with it, looking at everyone in the company and seeing who's comfortable and who's not. I'm very open about what the business needs and I'll always do what's right for it.'

WORKING WITH FAMILY

Holly: 'Working with family has been the making of us. I worked at one point with my father, mother, sister and cousin, not to mention a few people I'd grown up with since I was two years old. Sophie's sister, Claudia, helped us from the beginning with legal advice and now, eight years on, works for the business full time as our legal counsel. Working with family has all the upsides and not many down. But when you do have hard moments they are hard. My father was the finance director for seven years – he was also our mentor. It was a triangle – Robert, Sophie and me. It was tough for us all when the time came for him to retire. Things had moved on in the business so much that he knew it was time for a fresh perspective; this helped my humble mentor of a father make the difficult decision to stop working after forty-five years. I was quite panicky about how we would replace him. I was sure there would be lots of positives – new vision, new ways of doing things, classic commercial background and so on – but when would I get that fatherly pat on the back after a tricky meeting or conversation with an employee? We luckily found our new CFO (chief finance officer), who puts relationships first and that has helped enormously.'

Working with family can be wonderful for start-ups, as they will support you and often work harder for less money. Knowing you as well as they do, they should also understand your goals. But it also means that emotions can run high and when you move your business on to the next stage, they may not be the right people to bring with you.

Here's our advice for making it work with your family:

* In the workplace, family members are employees first and foremost. If they work for you, then they must have the fair and proper documentation in place.
* Take care not to treat family members more or less favourably than other staff.
* Manage your workforce with an even hand. Don't create biased hierarchies at work – family and staff must go by the same rules.
* Take care with job titles. As with any member of staff, anyone who works for you should have a clear role, direction and proper management.
* Argue in private. Just do. If you don't, staff may avoid telling you things they think you wouldn't want to hear, just to avoid causing a row.

PART TWO: DEVELOPMENT

Now that your administration is whistle-clean, we can look at the frankly more interesting engagement and development side of HR. This can mean a variety of things, from line management, setting clear objectives and career development plans right through to working out whether you want a fun, relaxed culture or a serious, formal environment for your team.

But before you can lead your team, you need to know your own personal motivations and drivers. You should have gleaned quite a bit about this from the previous chapter, in being honest about your strengths and weaknesses. This time, we want you to examine what the thorn in your side might be.

We think that anyone who seeks to build a business or successful career is motivated by something, whether that's fear, hunger for success, an absent parent or the teacher at school who told them they'd never amount to anything. Equally, it could be nothing more than the desire to give your family an annual holiday or a personal mission to get people recycling more efficiently. Identifying what that thing is can help you to maintain motivation when the going gets tough, as it inevitably will.

Before we ask you to think about your deepest personal drivers, we'll tell you our own.

Holly: 'Insecurity is my driver. Somehow, it stays with me, no matter what. I firmly believe in the mantra "Success is 1 per cent inspiration, 99 per cent perspiration" but then, I suppose, I would. As a child I suffered from dyslexia, low self-esteem and a low self-image because of weight problems, all of which culminated in my teen years with a long-term boyfriend who would put me down. I ended up marrying him (and divorced him a few years later), which tells you everything you need to know about how I felt about myself then.

'The dyslexia especially affected me. I think it's because it made even daily conversations hard and every single thing that I wrote had to be inspected for mistakes – I was constantly found wanting. Perhaps it's no coincidence that dyslexics are five times more likely to become entrepreneurs – they may not do well at school but they'll flourish in places that break the mould. I'm also pushed to succeed by my business teacher – I got an E for Business Studies. So I need to prove him wrong. And my grandfather, when I couldn't remember the months of the year when I was eight years old, told me that I would probably have a tough time "out there" but that everyone would still love me. Which was sweet if misguided. But these things are your drivers. My mum points out that I have to be grateful for these difficulties – I might not be where I am today without them.

'Now I know that the business is doing well, better than I ever dreamed, but with that comes a new set of insecurities driven by the fact that I have nearly 200 employees – soon to be 250, and 5,000 partners – which in no time at all will escalate to 10,000, relying on me to keep the company going strong. I constantly think about the opportunities we didn't take. I am never satisfied with where we are and put myself under pressure to go further, faster every day.

'Which means that essentially nothing has changed when it comes to me and my innermost self. I thought it would but it hasn't. The thing that most exhausts me is that I can't find my "off" switch. I always thought that the desire in me to build things would calm down but it hasn't. The way I think about it is that we are in such a fortunate position, doing something that has never been done before, we must take every opportunity. My fear is that we don't go fast enough and don't live up to the full potential of the business. It is all-consuming and has been ever since we began, there's been no tipping point – it was always like that and it probably always will be.

'However, knowing more about the way I work and what motivates me has helped me to keep perspective and manage the way I set my goals. I'm a "what if" person and that means I'm never going to say "Great! We've done it!" I know that can be annoying for the people around me but at least if they know that's how I am then their expectations won't be any different.

'Something else keeps me from relaxing and that's the fear that contentment might actually happen. If it did, I fear I'd coast a bit. Instead, I get out of bed every morning as worried and excited as I did when I first began. I've been surprised at that but that's about knowing yourself too. This is who I'm going to be for the rest of my life. I know that if I could I'd critique and improve my own coffin! I might as well get comfortable with it.'

Sophie: 'For some reason, I've always felt the need to write my own rule book and create my own territory. From the earliest age, being measured against and by people I didn't rate or believe in felt all wrong, dispiriting and sapped my confidence. I wasn't encouraged at school. I am deeply uncomfortable in a rigid institution and I wasn't happy at any of the several I tried out. I never felt as if I belonged. Sport cast me out – I was the chubby, unsporty one – so I was a physical misfit too. I had to practise shot put alone at the end of the field while everyone else did netball training! Forever after doing anything sporty felt fraudulent. Eventually I took control of that and now I can do a handstand push-up and I've run the London marathon, I reckon I'm proving it's the sports teacher that failed, not me.

'Adulthood was the goal for me. It would mean independence and choice. And that turned out to be true. Since I was a child, planning my job and how I'd buy my first flat, I also knew I wanted to have lots of children and it simply didn't occur to me not to work or to "marry money" to make it happen. I was very lucky to have a live-in role model because my mum was always a successful, ambitious woman – she's now a bestselling author but when I was growing up she was a journalist and she combined that with having a big, happy family.

'At the same time, the big story in our house was that my father's great dissatisfaction at working in a big corporation, tied to a good salary to support his ever-growing family, was going to end because he had the courage and vision to go it alone. From then on, we would proudly say "My dad has his own company" to anyone who asked. So I think that also set a little trigger off in my brain, that being tied to a corporate job meant frustration and sadness.

'There was no eureka moment that determined my path but rather a build-up of occurrences that led me to where I am now: from the corporate culture in advertising when the office politics felt like battles that weren't worth fighting to the desire to have a working life on my own terms once I'd had my children. I began to create a picture in my mind of what my job was going to have to look like and it was then I knew that setting up my own business was the only way to go.

'When Holly got in touch with me to see if I was willing to join forces with her, it was serendipitous timing. I think I've been proved right – as have so many of our small businesses – that your own business is the one that will deliver on your wider goals. It's a pattern that is replicated over and over. Know what you want – then go for it. And give thanks we live in a world that allows women not only to believe this but to make it happen.'

DAYS 9 TO 10 PRACTICAL EXERCISE:
BE YOUR OWN COACH FOR A DAY
allow: one and a half days

As a business owner or leader you should already be confident that you are good at making things happen. This probably means you have come to rely on your own abilities, determination and stamina to get things done.

Which is good.

You will also know about all those things you have put off, are ignoring or doing badly. But if those things are fundamental to the success of your business – such as finance or managing people – you need to address them as soon as possible.

Just as coaches help even top athletes improve their game, you can coach yourself to be better. One caveat: this only works if you are seriously prepared to make changes as to how you do things. That includes challenging long-held beliefs such as 'I'm no good at maths' or 'I'm painfully shy.'

1/ Plan your day of coaching

Allow yourself a day and choose it wisely. Choose a day when the business will be quiet – whether that's between Christmas and New Year or a Friday. You can break the day up into pieces too; most coaching sessions don't last more than a couple of hours. Think about where to meet with yourself – somewhere you can think undisturbed and where you will have Wi-Fi and refreshments. It needn't be your office – it could be a gallery or beautiful outside space, for inspiration. Before the session identify areas for development and self-improvement by doing the next two tasks in this list. Work out what the benefits for you will be to help your motivation.

2/ Gather feedback

Find people you have worked with to give some useful feedback on you, your business and even your future. Ask them questions such as: 'How do I react when something's gone well?' 'Am I happy with the achievement of a goal? Do I share this or keep it to myself?' Choose from your partner (business or personal), staff, suppliers and customers. Or ask people you admire.

If you are uncomfortable asking for feedback for your own personal development, tell them that it's for your business planning cycle. You can ask them one to one, in an email or through a quick online poll (come up with ten or so questions and let the site collate the responses for you).

If you tend to take things personally, ask someone to filter responses and summarise them, or even to ask the questions. But remember that anything negative is dynamite – because you can do something about it.

The information gathered here will shape your goals for your first session.

3/ Check your health

Are you in the best physical, mental and emotional condition to lead a business? What is your lifestyle like? Do you eat well, get exercise and have regular check-ups? Are there any medical matters that need attention? Or perhaps there are issues from your past or in your personal life that keep on popping into your head that you don't want to deal with? It's obvious but being in peak condition gives you an advantage.

Take action now if only because it makes real commercial sense. Visit the gym, see a nutritionist, your GP or a counsellor.

4/ The coaching day itself

Bring to your coaching session your feedback and goals, as well as your laptop and phone. Check nothing urgent requires your attention so that you can relax and focus.

Here are some questions to identify some actions for yourself around your development. They may seem repetitive but that is the intention. Write the answers down. Keep a separate list of actions or issues requiring follow-up.

* What is the next milestone for my business/my career?
* What are the issues that are stopping this from happening?
* What makes these issues – i.e. things that matter or niggle – now?
* Who is responsible for these issues or problems?
* How important are they on a scale of one to ten?
* How much energy do I have to find a solution on a scale of one to ten?
* What are the implications on my business/my career if I let things carry on as they are?
* What have I already tried?
* If I managed to solve this problem, how would my business/job feel?
* What is standing in the way of the ideal outcome?
* How much of the responsibility for fixing this is mine?
* What early signs are there that things might be starting to improve?
* What are the options for further action?
* What criteria will I use to judge the different options?
* Which option seems the best one against those criteria?
* What is my first/next step?
* Who else might I involve?
* When will I take action?

5/ Understand your personality

Take a professional profile test as we recommended in the Honesty Diary. If you didn't do it then, do it now. We didn't have one done until we had been running the business for a few years and we wish we hadn't waited. Personality profiles are powerful tools for entrepreneurs. Using the knowledge we gleaned, particularly of how our two personalities combined, helped us when it came to recruiting and developing other team members.

6/ Your existing team

Make a list of your existing team - whether in your business or department - together with their strengths and weaknesses. Rate them and identify what you'd miss if they left as well as what you'd like them to improve. Then try to identify how you can help them move forward. Don't be afraid to seek the help of an independent HR professional to do this with you.

It is also worthwhile (and fun!) to use the Belbin Team Roles questionnaire (see The Directory) to identify the team roles you and your key staff play. It's a simple exercise that will help identify the types of people that are missing from your workplace.

7/ Your action list

You will now have an action list to break down further into clear manageable tasks. Identify what you can do independently, what resources you have or need, who else will need to get involved and, most importantly, when you intend to do it. By now, you may identify that a business coach or someone you trust to support you will be useful in that process.

Capture your action points under three headings:
* My development actions
* Resources needed
* Target for completion

Keep front of mind that you have invested in yourself today and, just like your business, you need a return on that investment. Follow through and deliver the actions you've committed to. Not just the easy fun stuff, but the things you feel a slight dread about too. Review your action list regularly but don't feel despondent if you miss a few deadlines. Reschedule and keep on moving. Think how good you will feel when they are sorted.

Holly: 'I've been doing a lot of work with a coach to bring the management team together. What it's helped me to understand is that until you know who you are and what makes you tick, you cannot work at full tilt. Without that knowledge you only know you're stressed and what you're stressed about, which doesn't really help.'

So that's you, understanding your own motivation, strengths, goals and hurdles. Now you have put yourself in a position to start doing the same for your team.

WHAT MOTIVATES AND GETS THE
BEST OUT OF YOUR PEOPLE?

Just because you feel spun out with excitement about something, it won't necessarily be enough to drive the people you work with. Passion can be contagious but the skill is to translate that passion into something to which others can relate.

Holly: 'When we moved to our big new offices we were suddenly all separated and one of the things that happened was that the tech team felt isolated. I also came to realise that we had to change the way in which they were managed: they are artists. We weren't treating them as we did the creatives and yet we should have been. They're creating code and it may not be a pretty picture, but it's a pretty algorithm. The barrier between tech teams and the rest of the company is commonplace in business today, yet technology is the lifeblood of any brand in the twenty-first century. We had to do a lot of work to overcome the void that had grown over the years.'

The business driver that works for us and also motivates our team is the mission to help partners. In getting things right or done well for notonthehighstreet.com we're not just enjoying our own success, we are enabling thousands of small businesses to grow and do well. That's a great feeling and it's unifying too. We devised our values acronym together, as a team, around that driver so that we all know what it means in the workplace and how we all work together to make it happen. Every one of our staff is committed to being able to say it: I AM REAL (Instinctive, Ambitious, Meaningful, Real, Exceptional, Analytical, Loving).

It's not always going to be a carrot at the end of a stick that motivates your staff, either as individuals or as a team. Autonomy, mastery and purpose: these things matter as much, if not more, than salary. Paying someone more takes the issue of money off the table – and if someone feels seriously underpaid, it will be an issue – but in isolation, it won't get you better performance. In fact, guaranteed bonus payments can often have the opposite effect, especially if everyone gets the same regardless of their contribution or effort.

Instead, research has shown that if you give people clear goals that have meaning – a real purpose – they will work harder because they see the point. That research also shows that if you reward them with autonomy when they achieve those goals – freedom to work and strive in the way they feel comfortable and empowered – they feel more entrepreneurial, are happier and more effective. And give them the opportunity to learn, to master new skills, to grow their knowledge, and they will feel they are personally progressing too.

To work these principles, you can take very practical, simple steps with each employee. The most important thing is that people know what is expected of them and what their role is. Your business needs you to lead and manage people in a way that helps them understand the part they play in achieving its goals. Before you can communicate any goals, you will need to have defined them yourself – you will have done much of this on Days 6 and 7. Be very clear that you know exactly where your business is going and what you want to achieve in the next three, six and twelve months.

Once this is done, you can start communicating what's expected of each member of staff. The first part of that will be their job description, which should have formed an integral part of the hiring process. This document is worth spending time on, defining the scope of the role and where it might lead. The most powerful conversation you can have with a member of your staff is fleshing out this role description and helping make it happen, by identifying experience they need to get or things they need to do. Don't overpromise or you may under-deliver, but you should both be clear about what you think might be possible. Knowing that is pretty motivational – every employee values being treated as an individual and having a boss who is honest.

The second part of communicating what's expected is to discuss their more immediate, specific goals. You need to do this initially as a group, the whole department, or even company. Then, subsequently, at an individual level.

Imagine a triangle divided horizontally into three parts: the top pointed part is the business goals, the middle part is the team goals and the bottom part is the individual goals. There is a clear line of sight between goals and activity.

At that top, pointed level, communicate through a group presentation, perhaps tied in with a social occasion. Go into as much detail as you are prepared to share – the more you share the more engaged your team will be. Try not to keep back more than you have to – there should be confidentiality statements in your employment contracts to make you comfortable doing this.

On an individual level, meetings should take place regularly. Get into a habit of giving each member of your team regular direction and clarity about what you want. Then give feedback on how well it's going, in a continuous cycle of feedback and further direction. That direction should be SMART: Specific, Measurable, Achievable, Realistic and Time-bound.

It's essential to make time to talk to individuals regularly and *face to face* – short weekly and monthly chats, plus a fuller chat once or twice a year. Plan this bigger session as a one-to-one motivational event – if time allows, take them out for a meal, or to meet someone that can help their career, or where you can talk in an inspiring space. This care is appreciated and can really make people feel valued and loyal; email and texts have a place but don't overuse them.

Keep records (or get your employees to do so for your approval) of discussions and agreed areas of focus. Invest in a simple online system that enables you to keep permanent centralised, shared records. Allowing employees to log on and update aims and achievements is a great way to work collaboratively, flexibly and in tune with your business cycle. They can add documents, notes and comments – far better than a formal appraisal system; instead it creates that ongoing feedback loop where you interact with your employees in a natural way. In this social-media world, this approach reflects the way people now routinely update personal information. Keep in mind that there is no legal requirement to have an appraisal system so this is purely about having a system to manage your employees without creating too much extra work or unnecessary paperwork.

Direct, manage and motivate your staff in this way and although you'll find that initially you spend more time briefing people, this will soon be replaced by the pleasure of praising great results from a team that really understands what you want and is ready to push the bar even higher.

What are the best things about hiring and employing people?
And what are the worst?

My 1st Years: Learning new skills from your staff is something that not many bosses would admit to, but sometimes as a boss you're the clever one for hiring people with better skill sets than you in certain areas.

Ellie Ellie: The best thing about hiring someone is to be able to share the Ellie Ellie dream, being able to share the success and the journey with young and talented individuals during a time where employment is hard to find. The worst is the paperwork! As much as employing someone relieves you from a workload, it also creates work! Contracts, training, policies, holidays, sickness, codes of conduct, pensions – they all take up time but it's part of the responsibility.

Pearl and Earl: In our first year we grew too quickly and ran out of cash. We had to make two people redundant. It was awful and at Christmas too. We have been much more cautious since and everyone now knows they need to be able to turn their hand to anything, which means we are small but efficient. There are no politics, the office is fun, we have really good coffee machines (all important stuff) and offer all our staff the same incentives from healthcare to free lunches in December – all things the staff have voted for. I want Pearl and Earl to be not just successful but a really cool place to work. Incentives that don't cost the earth are enough to keep people focused and happy; it's an extra juggle that you don't have to deal with when it's just you but it pays off in staff loyalty.

Sophia Victoria Joy: Handing over the responsibility for something only you have ever done is very difficult. Learning to trust that others will then do it right, as fast and as efficiently without any mistakes is the toughest bit.

Delightful Living: Putting a team together is very rewarding when you get it right. Seeing employees develop and learn new skills and the contribution they bring to the team as a whole is very satisfying. But managing people can also be a big headache. Investing time and energy into training staff, being patient and accommodating of individual needs and personal circumstances can be challenging at times. And when you've found that perfect team member and they leave it can have a big impact on the rest of the team and the business as a whole.

Do you have any tips? Things you wish you'd known?
How do you share any pain or difficulty that
comes from people management?

Oakdene Designs: Get a good system to record the hours employees work and work out what you owe them. Running the payroll used to take a lot of time, but after making some spreadsheets on Excel it has become a much easier process. Fortunately, my accountant is a good friend who has plenty of experience in running a medium-sized business, so I will often talk to him about any difficulties.

Ellie Ellie: Don't try and do it all yourself when it comes to HR. Get in the experts – it may be expensive but it will be more expensive if you hire the wrong person. Make sure you spend time with your staff on a personal level and introduce clear performance reviews and objectives to make sure you are getting the most out of them and they are getting the most out of you. And trust your gut – it's always right!

Sophia Victoria Joy: I would have hired staff much sooner and invested that time in sharing the workload. A few days of training may put you back a little but it will save weeks in the future. We always work to the strengths of our team. There are days where I can see struggles. I put it all down on paper and match jobs to best suit the team members.

Confidence

'Whether you think you can or think
you can't – you are right.'

HENRY FORD

DAYS 11 TO 14

What we mean by confidence; unlocking your creativity;
the importance of preparation; learning to negotiate;
exercises to boost your confidence.

Now that you have established your drivers and set your goals, you need to press the button and get on with achieving them. If you're hesitating at the start line, it'll be for one simple reason: a lack of confidence.

The most common method to tackle this is to front it up – make it *look* as if you know what you're doing and eventually the mind will catch up with the body. We're masters of this. When we began notonthehighstreet.com, we were as green as fresh mint but we knew that if we were to persuade partners to join, we had to look like a mature and grown-up business. We projected this by sending beautiful folders of information to even the smallest of potential business partners; when we first needed stories in the press, we focused on the national broadsheets and leading women's glossy magazines to give us a much bigger platform than the size of the business merited. We believed that the image of success would go part of the way in actually creating that success. This works – creating a buzz is always a good thing to do. But we're not talking about marketing and PR here. We're talking about how you operate every day.

We were lucky. When it came to our business, we always had genuine confidence. Even though we were technically putting our houses on the

your confidence

line in order to get notonthehighstreet.com up and running – we could only just meet our mortgage payments and we had absolutely zero savings so any squeeze was a huge risk – it somehow never felt as if we were truly compromising the security of our families. We were completely confident and very excited – perhaps we don't seem to feel the fear in the same way that others do. We don't know if it's rooted in our childhoods, or our characters, or simply the fact that we have always totally and utterly believed in notonthehighstreet.com. But no matter how alarming things have got – and sometimes they have been very alarming indeed – we've always believed that it will come right in the end.

However, when it comes to personal confidence … that's a whole different ball game going on, right there. As each award was placed on our shelves, or a new employee was taken on, or a turnover goal was hit, we were surprised that we still felt the same. Would there ever be a day when we could have a meeting with the big guns and not worry that the papers we were holding would so obviously be shaking in our hands?

As is so often true of women, our level of confidence was rarely in line with what it should have been – it's as if the roller-coaster story of building the business has a contrasting, invisible roller coaster of confidence, self-belief or the lack of.

For instance, early on, there were times when we'd be dying inside, scared witless at realising we were almost bust but having to go all out with media interviews and industry talks.

Sophie: 'I distinctly remember doing an interview with a women's big glossy magazine that we'd been trying to secure for quite some time.

And now it was on. While I'd been waiting for the journalist to call, Holly, Robert and I had been looking, again, at the numbers. They were horrific. We were in such big trouble it felt hardly worth even staying in the office that afternoon. We were both white as sheets, very upset and in shock. Then the phone rang and I had to switch into successful entrepreneur mode. I couldn't bear to stay in the office, so I went out and walked the cold, miserable backstreets around our office. "Just how amazing is it?" said the journalist. "I bet you can hardly believe it." I could barely speak ... but thought, believe what? She went on: "You've done so well. Notonthehighstreet.com is everywhere. How does it feel?" And so I dug deeper than ever, talked the talk and spent the next twenty minutes prattling effusively about how truly wonderful it all was and how happy our staff, customers and partners were. It felt like stepping out of a car crash to do a gloriously musical tap dance, complete with rousing vocals and big finish.'

Yet there were other moments, at the top of the confidence roller coaster, when we were walking on air, masters of the universe, only not everyone quite knew it yet. There was a stage of the business when we weren't looking too hot – we weren't exactly famous, numbers were a bit paltry, people didn't know about us yet and those patronising questions would come at drinks parties – but inside we were singing, on fire, so sure of what was coming, what a massive business we were going to be. You might not know about us now, sunshine, we'd think, but you sure as hell will.

Even the most successful people you know will have suffered from 'imposter syndrome' at some point – the belief that one is pulling the wool over everyone's eyes – we know we have. But you can get over this if you identify what you're good at and what you're not. Go deeper than your accounting skills or ability to draw a perfect circle. Allow for your weaknesses too – 'I can't do this, so I'm going to bring someone in' – and move on.

There's a difference between imposter syndrome and recognising that you still need to punch your weight. Humility and a genuine appraisal of your skills are what are called for here. If you're feeling unsure about where you are, ask yourself: who has put you in that position and do you respect their decisions? Who else occupies the same kind of space as you and what do you think of them? Alongside this, consider the precise skills and experience that are necessary for your work or business and be honest if you don't have them. You won't be able to keep faking it.

If as a boss you're suffering from imposter syndrome, you cannot let on to your team. It will undermine their confidence in you and at that point, leadership fails. What you need to keep in mind is that being a good leader is as much, if not more, about asking the right questions as it is about having the right answers. Focus on direction rather than direct answers.

The good news is that things *have* changed in the years since we first began and we both feel a deeper level of confidence and self-assuredness. With work, and time, it comes.

Sophie: 'At the beginning, 90 per cent of the confidence I had was in the business. I knew it was exceptional and was able to visualise completely how it should be. There was, for us, a curious alignment of the stars in that the combination of skills that we had accrued at that time – the knowledge of small businesses, writing, brand development, ability to sell, advertising, clients, production, quality control and early technology – suddenly all became relevant at once. This made us feel bulletproof. It was a one-in-a-million situation and that was a rush. It felt amazing and right to be doing what we were doing.

'As the business grew, I realised that without the professional management training that I might have had with a more textbook career path, I needed to work hard and learn more in order to maintain that confidence. My background had worked perfectly at the truly entrepreneurial stage of the business when vision, lateral thinking and sheer drive are what you need most, but as the business grew that changed. Naturally, as your business grows and evolves, so should you and so should the work you do for it. But it can knock your personal confidence, no matter how much you believe in what you're doing.

'Deep down, you need to remember that your confidence is there, and why. Even when I felt on less solid ground, I always felt very confident in having high emotional intelligence. Being able to read and understand people, quickly and accurately. At first I wondered if that was something that might not be relevant in this newly formalised workplace and it knocked me back a bit. But then our goals became more focused on emotionally based and measured skills and products – PR, publicity, brand value, culture, creative work, personal development and motivations at work – and those skills of mine became very important, even taking over from the more practical ones I'd previously drawn on in the early days. I knew it was critical to the business, I felt strong and sure in that role and my confidence returned.'

So we began to recognise that the areas where we had confidence were still relevant – essential, in fact. It was the application of them that was different. In short, we remembered to play to our strengths, just as we had at the beginning.

Holly: 'I've always felt that creativity is my strength and yet I was the one, for example, handling departments such as finance with my father. Ultimately, I realised it wasn't about my number-crunching skills – they don't really exist – it was about my instinct, my good eye and my ability to measure. Bringing all those things together was not only something I could do well, it was just what the company needed. And I was then able to translate that into some highly successful fundraising, not through my maths, but through my vision and belief, which Sophie will always tell you are legendary!'

Keep in mind that you don't need to shout loudly about the things you can do – confidence shouldn't be a face-off as it sometimes is. Instead, work out where you need confidence, and where you need other things: empathy, preparation, self-belief, knowledge. These are the seeds that will help you and your business bloom.

Holly: 'Knowing who I am has given me more than confidence. Now I can trust my gut reaction because it got me here. I know now that I have to have *balance*, that's my key word. Balance between my roles as a mother, a wife and as a CEO, giving time to each. Balance at work between building the business and feeding my creativity. Balance between giving and taking.'

DAYS 11 TO 12 PRACTICAL EXERCISE:
HOW TO IDENTIFY THE REASONS WHY
AND THE WAYS IN WHICH YOU
ARE CONFIDENT

allow: across two days – thinking time is important here –
clear spaces (where you can) in your working day

Picture this scenario. You are standing looking at a bonfire. The bonfire
is neither good nor bad. Put your hand into the flames. Now it is bad,
right? Yet if you were toasting a marshmallow and getting warm on a cold
night it would be good. The bonfire didn't change. Our relationship with
it, however, did. The same is true of our relationship with confidence. It is
why people reference false confidence and overconfidence/arrogance.
It shapes our judgement, and yet whichever way our judgement goes, it
doesn't make it right!

So let us come at our relationship with confidence another way. Do you
know that it's your attitude to yourself and your abilities that most affects
your relationship with confidence?

1/ Do you feel as if you, personally, are able to do it – whatever
your current challenge is – or is it something that you believe 'other
people' do?

2/ Do you know that you can make it happen or do you suspect that no
matter what you do it won't work out?

3/ Do you truly know that you deserve all the success that is possible? Or do you suspect you are a fraud? That somewhere down the line you will be found out or even that you simply don't deserve it?

If you answer positively to these questions, away you go! If negatively, you need to think more closely about the reasons why. It will help to imagine that you have been instructed that 'you must do it'. You can even introduce a consequence – if you don't do it, there will be a negative impact on you/someone close to you. What then? How do you feel now? Notice what happens … you find a way. Keep working at these questions over the two days.

SUCCESS AND CONFIDENCE

Does success equal confidence? Of course it does. Not *because* you're a success but because you overcame great difficulty to get there. In fact, if you feel success came too easily that can, conversely, knock your confidence. If you don't understand how it happened, you may feel it was just a fluke or a lucky break, something that may not happen again or could easily be taken away from you. This is also partly why it's important to measure your successes (and failures) at every opportunity, so that you can monitor not only what has happened in the business but why. You'll most likely understand then that you were responsible for it. But always *own* your success. It was you who did this, no one else, so make it part of who you are.

Holly: 'Confidence comes out of the nasty things you are forced to deal with. I gave up smoking. I never thought I could take control of it; turns out, I could. I got my weight under control. I am exercising. Then I dealt with the "friend" who had made me feel worthless for the last twenty years. The realisation that last year these things were prevalent, were worries on my mind, and that this year they're not – that's amazing. I tackled things that had been under my skin for years and *that* gave me confidence.'

We want you to be the best of who you are. And we believe that you can do whatever you need to do, if you find the right way to do it. Holly is a creative person but she was key to raising four rounds of funding. How did she do it? It wasn't a degree in crunching numbers. It was her flair for visualising the future of the company and getting that vision across in a way that inspired and excited our investors. We worked hard to rigorously test our financial forecasts and that didn't come easily but we knew we had to do it, so we did. Remember, your biggest competitive advantage is always going to be working hard and if you have done that, you should allow yourself to feel confident about moving on to the next stage.

CONFIDENCE IN PRACTICE: NEGOTIATION

Negotiation is an area where we believe that *not* being a natural can actually help. It is possible to study and learn the art of negotiation. Having felt unease in the past may even help, you will know how uncomfortable the other side is feeling, no matter how much they act the opposite.

Nor will you always be negotiating about money. In fact, we've found that some of our most key negotiations have been about creative work; finding a place where everyone is happy and comfortable with what we've needed to do creatively.

Here are our best negotiating tactics.

Preparation
As with anything, preparation is your killer advantage. Do your homework: know where you can compromise and where you mustn't budge and know your opposition too. Knowing and understanding what's important to the other side is critical.

Belief
While memorising the figures is good practice, it's the emotional side of negotiation that makes the difference to a successful outcome. First, from your side, you need to utterly and completely believe in what you're saying and offering in order to close the transaction. If you don't take time to turn your mind round to why you truly believe in what you are offering, you will lose the deal. Negotiation is not tricks and clever dressing up – it is based on being genuine and positive energy. If you don't believe, nor will they.

Thanks but no thanks
Make sure you give yourself all the reasons why you do not need the deal. Even if you really need the deal and everything rests on it! Take the time out to come up with other options that you have and make sure you understand that they are possible. You need to truly believe that you do not need it. Your vibe will be read as genuine and give the other party a true indication that you are ready to walk away. The person who needs it least is in control.

Give it away

Build the deal so that you have things you can give away. Everyone likes to believe they have won in some way. Make sure you are giving away things that you do not mind releasing. It needs to be genuine so that everyone feels what they receive is worth something. Make it win-win.

Feelings not numbers

Remember your own emotional insight; remember that it's as much about how people feel as what the numbers say. The negotiators will need to go back to their team with their heads held high, while you do the same. That's the *art* of negotiation.

Holly: 'Back to the story of the deal that nearly killed me [see pages 23-4]. After the crisis call there was a moment where the whole deal rested on my shoulders. It needed the best of me and the best of my business ability. I had to remind myself of the fact that everything in life – if you trace it back to its true source – is powered by love or fear. I had to find the source of why the deal was about to break and realised that it was all around fear. So after a good night's sleep and a glass of wine with friends, I got back on that phone and tackled the issue head on.

'I made sure that I did not sound desperate (remember to negotiate only when you have visualised walking away) and put a plan to the other party that had protection for them, if their fears came true, but honoured the deal that we had negotiated over the last three months, if what I had been promising came true. I used the best of my business knowledge, language and skill but also made sure that my bubbly personality shone through. Twenty-four hours had passed and what was pretty much a broken deal suddenly became a conversation about the best date to sign the papers!'

QUIET CONFIDENCE

There are those of us who are never going to be brash and ballsy. You might have to put in the hours, understand your subject, prepare, know your subject and be rather more strategic – choose your battles, in other words. Avoid your confidence being knocked by staying well clear of the arenas that at best are never going to make you feel good or at worst might even do you permanent damage. Trying to be something you're not is the fastest route to screwing up.

Sophie: 'At one point, I was dealing with a very complicated and tough issue. There was a meeting I was dreading and I said to someone, "I know I'm going to have to go in and tackle this head on. Bury my fear and just deal with it in a very upfront way." I expected the person I said this to, someone I trust and respect enormously, to say yes, be brave and toughen up. Because that's what people always say, isn't it? Instead, she said: "Why would you do that? You've achieved everything you've achieved by being you and true to yourself. You've always done things the way that feels right to you – why would you abandon that at such an important time? You've done all the groundwork, you know exactly what you need to know and the result you want. It's more important than ever that you deal with this as you – otherwise you'll feel weak and unconfident." So I went in as myself. And she was right.'

PRACTICE MAKES CONFIDENT

That doesn't mean you should always stay inside your comfort zone. Far from it. We do things every day that make us squirm, feel nervous, exposed. But we do them. We pick up the phone and say what has to be said or walk into a room and make a speech, and each time it's a little bit easier than the last because we are always building on our skills and experience.

In a business situation, there's one sure-fire way to confidence and that's preparation. Thinking through a presentation or meeting that you are nervous about will help you be ready to face any outcome. Spend as much time as you can anticipating all the questions you could be asked and have all the answers ready. Know your business inside out – you probably do anyway but make sure the figures are ironclad and the schedule rigorous. Have 'soft launches' with a trusted colleague or friend before you enter a boardroom. Like a well-known comedian testing out their Edinburgh Fringe material on a regional stage or two, ask someone to be your own personal devil's advocate, picking holes in your argument and asking terrifyingly tricky questions.

Know your stuff and the nerves will diminish.

Sophie: 'My daughter Honor is fifteen and exactly like me when it comes to confidence – she'll take time to build her confidence in public speaking. She sometimes comes to hear me give talks and the last time she asked me afterwards, "How do you do that? I know you feel like I do really." My answer: "Because I've done it over and over again, hundreds of times. You do the things that you're afraid of as many times as you have to, until they become normal, and then even if it's scary, you don't stop to think. You just get on with it."'

DAY 13 PRACTICAL EXERCISE:
CONFIDENCE IN ACTION – LEADERSHIP
allow: two hours

It can be hard to follow the above advice when you're acting as a mentor to others. When asked to come up with a solution or set a task, quiet confidence may not be the ticket. But that's okay. If we change the rules of engagement, so that we don't always talk about confidence – the word that signals the testosterone-fuelled kind – but talk instead about being prepared, being empathetic and being insightful, well, doesn't that hearten you? Doesn't it make you think – yes, *that* I can do?

Dr John C. Maxwell identified the five levels of leadership, a now well-established descriptor of the stages and parameters one goes through – or aims for! – as one moves up. We like his work because he clearly shows that the more successful and influential a person is, the less they rely on vocal, forceful leadership or explicit demonstrations of strength and the more they rely on their inherently powerful presence, their natural influence and what they stand for.

LEVEL ONE:
Position
People follow you because they have to.

LEVEL TWO:
Permission
People follow you because they want to.

LEVEL THREE:
Production
People follow you because of what you have done for the organisation.

LEVEL FOUR:
People Development
People follow you because of what you have done for them.

LEVEL FIVE:
Pinnacle
People follow you because of who you are and what you represent.

Spend time thinking about what kind of leader you are, where you feel your inner confidence and display your outer confidence, and how you might move up a level or two in ways that might surprise you and the people around you.

Something that's worth mentioning here is that while all of us draw strength from the support of friends and colleagues, sometimes it is very important not to chase the popular vote. We've both done our fair share of this. As CEO, Holly has to make some tough decisions and the one thing we both know is that business isn't always a popularity contest. At times, Sophie too could be a bit of a scary boss – if something needed to be done in those early days, it had to be done fast and she brooked no argument. In the short term, making yourself unpopular is fine. What does matter, however, that you have respect from your colleagues and the bottom line is that only a confident leader commands respect.

CONFIDENCE IN THE PEOPLE WE WORK WITH

As we said earlier, when it came to notonthehighstreet.com, we've always had every confidence in the business itself – yes, even the ballsy kind. There was nothing quiet about our belief that we could make it succeed if we worked hard enough.

We've also been very lucky with our team and as the business has grown our confidence has included our belief in the people who work for us. But that's not to say that we haven't made mistakes now and then, whether that's been setting uphelpful goals or not matching skill sets to a task correctly.

When it comes to the business, we need to know every single person in it, from web designer to customer service manager. As we've grown, we can't always do that personally any more, but we stay in tune and connected through our leadership team. We do this not only because it makes for a happy team, but because it is vital that we know exactly how to push and challenge them, without asking them to be something they're not.

Sophie: 'Holly shares her vision with the staff. She's more the one to encourage ballsy confidence and instil it in others. I tend to tease it out of people, give people the space and tools to find their own kind of confidence, perhaps by asking them what they think a solution might be or asking how I can support them in achieving it'

A lack of confidence in the work you're doing can come sometimes from a lack of direction. It may be that you simply need a little steering in the right direction. In these circumstances, prioritise what needs to be done.

Help your team to feel less overwhelmed by their long list of goals and things to do by giving them perspective on the bigger picture.

BIGGER BUSINESS = CONFIDENCE IN OTHERS

Looking back, the confidence shifts were inevitable for both of us as notonthehighstreet.com grew to a size where we couldn't do everything ourselves. Three years ago we took on some very senior and capable members of staff and were working closely with them. It felt epic and it was. We had been doing so much, it was constant but we felt on fire. As bosses we also felt very needed – if something went wrong, we could fix it. We were very involved in a lot of things. But ultimately that was unsustainable. Our home lives suffered and we were tired beyond belief. It was at that point we recognised we needed a senior management team. We were dealing with bigger and bigger numbers and suddenly it was apparent we needed five people to do the one job we had been trying to do ourselves. But once we got them in, we had to manage them and that was inevitably a challenge.

Sophie: 'These new leaders rightly had strong, clear views and I needed to think about how I was going to work confidently with that. I drew on advice that had been given to me early on in my career – when I was first experiencing management and leadership – which was simply to listen and learn as much as I possibly could, to take in a full range of perspectives, because then you're equipped to make your own choices when met with strong opinions. In short, have a view. Know the rules so you can break them. In this way, I looked to our new staff and learned from them, but I also became more sure of my own views and decisions.'

The point is that as you grow with the business you're in, you may gain confidence in some areas and lose it in others – that's what happened to us. But this is a good thing. When it comes to your business, it's not about the familiar, it shouldn't be. You're not doing a very good job if you're not constantly getting pulled into unrecognisable places. Go with it.

Fortunately, in time we learned to learn from this new set of colleagues – our management team – who we admire and trust. We love being able to say, 'Guess what? We have a COO now, and he's done all this before. Let's ask him!'

CONFIDENCE IN PRACTICE:
THE 'THREE BEFORE ME' RULE

In education, teachers will typically encourage their students to apply the 'three before me' rule. That is, the student must try to find the answer in at least three different ways – whether that's looking up the answer in a book, making a calculated guess or looking back over notes – before asking the teacher for the solution. This is a good principle for business leaders too.

Constantly giving answers to your team is, in any case, short-sighted as it will only undermine their own self-belief that they have the ability to find the solution themselves. At notonthehighstreet.com our senior management set their own objectives – they know what our goals are and we are happy to leave it in their hands. As someone moves up the career scale, their level of empowerment changes and as their boss you need to acknowledge that and work with it.

DAY 14 PRACTICAL EXERCISE:
THE CONFIDENCE TEST
allow: two hours

No cheating yourself. Answer honestly. Those answers that lie deep down within you may be the hardest to face but will bring the greatest release when you do. Dare to do it.

Using work as the context:

✳ What would be the type of environment that would bring out the absolute best in you, that you would leap out of bed to get to and would look back over your shoulder to on your way out?

✳ What are the things that you do that give you the greatest rush of energy?

✳ What are the skills that you either love using the most or seriously cannot wait to get?

✳ What things do you need to believe in and have others share with you to make dreams happen?

✳ What really is important to you when it comes to work and why?

✳ Is there any team, brand or organisation that you would happily associate yourself with that is almost a representation of who you are?

✳ Is it possible that you could leave a legacy that stands beyond any personal achievement through what you are contributing to?

If you can line up these things, you will fly. If you can line these up with your business activity, both it and you will fly! Nothing will stop you or be too problematic or hard. If one or more of these questions does not fit with your business venture, that is where you focus to check it is possible to align it and you. And notice what happens when you can align it.

WHAT CONFIDENCE CAN DO

We have discussed the merits of quiet confidence and admitted those areas where we don't feel fully confident ourselves, or talked about times where we came dangerously close to a confidence crisis and had to fight to overcome it. Despite those moments and in spite of our belief that a whispered, steely confidence can be as strong as a ballsy, smash-it-out-of-the-park confidence – different times call for different kinds – we do believe it is important to nurture and build confidence. It is, ultimately, necessary for success.

Here's why:

Confidence is liberating
If you tackle one thing successfully, you will find that you keep on going, riding the crest of the wave. Often, the things that cause you stress are those that you are scared of dealing with and hence recur year after year. If your business isn't going well, sometimes you have to ask yourself if something is chipping at your confidence and preventing you from moving

forward? Could it be a friend that puts you down? An unsupportive member of your family? Your own feelings about your appearance, health or fitness? An unhappy event from the past that has never been resolved? Smashing that issue could be the thing that frees you and allows you to take brave, bold steps with your business. No business ever grew without taking risks and if you are playing safe in order to minimise your fear and stress levels, then you and your business will be stuck.

Confidence unlocks creativity

Only when you are unafraid of going wrong or saying the wrong thing, will you find the most creative solutions to your problems.

Sophie: 'I've always been good at coming up with creative or innovative ideas and this is partly borne of the fact that I feel confident in that area. When it comes to this, I know how those unswervingly confident people feel. It just comes easily to me, like riding downhill on a bicycle, as my mother used to say. I enjoy it, the ideas flow and I don't worry about anyone calling the rubbish ideas out because I know I have plenty more good ones up my sleeve. That piece of knowledge about myself is so important because it gives confidence in other things.'

Somehow, with creativity, we can be too shy. As Winston Fletcher, author of *Seven Keys to Superefficiency*, said to Sophie once: 'When it comes to creativity, we are our own worst censors.' We have been very lucky to have each other to bounce ideas around, both good and bad. A supportive environment will give you the freedom to say the 'wrong' thing, which will lead you eventually to the 'right' place. Remember to offer that kind of support to those close to you and do not scorn what at first sounds like an off-the-wall solution.

How confident are you? How has your
confidence changed in the lifetime of your business?
What gives you confidence? And what knocks it?

Becky Broome: Confidence is a big issue in business. My motto
has always been 'If you don't have confidence in yourself, why should
anyone else?' That has always helped me to stay positive and confident
in business. Don't get me wrong – it can be very hard to stay positive
and confident if your business is struggling to get off the ground but
confidence can help you make difficult choices or help you head bravely
in a new direction. Businesses evolve and change just as the world
constantly changes; you have to have the confidence to adapt.

Highland Angel: I'm quite a quiet person, but I think I'm probably
more confident now. Having to make decisions and demands on behalf
of the business has forced me to be more outgoing, and I'm more likely
now to get on and do something without worrying about what people
will think. Seeing the business grow and getting positive feedback from
customers helps give you confidence that you are doing something right.
Sadly, rude and angry customers have the opposite effect! Luckily we
don't get too many, but when someone does complain you have to step
back and remember that it's not aimed at you personally.

Ellie Ellie: When I was younger I was always the shortest, youngest-
looking in the class so I had to have confidence in order for me to be
noticed and I still carry this need for confidence around with me now.
Being a young, petite female who doesn't necessarily dress in corporate

business clothing, I do get judged by the way I look and that is one of the most frustrating things in the business world. They soon change their opinion of me once I start talking and that's really all down to confidence in myself and my ability. I always believe in everything I do, every product we have, every member of staff and it is this belief that leads to my confidence. That's not to say my confidence is 100 per cent and to be honest I wouldn't ever want it to be, there's always room to grow and you must allow for that. The moment you become complacent is the moment your business stops growing. I had dedicated my whole life to education and training myself to become a designer – my childhood ambition – only to find things didn't work out quite as I had planned. I couldn't find a job and was back working at my local Marks and Spencer where I had worked since I was a teenager – it was heartbreaking. After three years I still hadn't found a design job, I had no money and was living back home with my mum. I decided to give it all up and went travelling for a year. I always had confidence in my ability to become successful; I just didn't at that stage have the personal confidence to go for it. I felt scared of failure but I also felt scared of success. Travelling taught me that I had the confidence to do anything I set out to do.

Pearl and Earl: I am naturally confident, but have lost some over the years. My confidence was fierce at the beginning but after our honeymoon period, you have to keep the cash and product innovation going once the initial shine of a new company has worn off, so it got knocked quite a bit. Everyone wants something new – and balancing this with your cash is tough. Buying a 'dog' (bad product) is not a habit you can afford to get into and production planning at Christmas is always a nailbiter! I feel now the perfect balance is confidence with instinct backed up with fact. So not overly cocky (data is treasure) but still leaving time and space to trust that instinct that got you started in the first place.

Sophia Victoria Joy: Seeing a new idea become a bestseller is the best feeling in the world. This is where most of my confidence stems from. When a new idea does not work out my confidence is knocked; however, this actually pushes me further to address the problem and so I eventually get to a stronger result.

Money talks

'Money was never a big motivation for me, except as a way to keep score. The real excitement is playing the game.'

DONALD TRUMP

DAYS 15 TO 18

Learning the language; removing the fear of money.

We need to talk about money. We know this can be hard. People are either afraid of money, in that they fear the power it wields if not the people who control their access to it; or they worry that merely wanting it makes them avaricious and greedy. But money is what keeps the plates spinning. It's important that we don't avoid the conversation when it needs to be had. Addressing the financial aspects of your business should not be an emotional minefield but the start of a strategic, practical plan to help it thrive.

In this chapter, we're going to look at the practicals of financial planning, how profitable productivity means more than cutting costs (though that matters too) and we'll also be getting into the stuff that's more personal.

Business owners should always be looking to the next level – making the leap from producing enough money to keep the business alive to growing big profits – and we want to help you achieve that mental jump, as well as give you the language you need to talk the talk.

There's no question that money is a determining factor in success. Those who are earning a salary will measure their pay against that of their colleagues or peers and judge accordingly whether or not they are doing well. A business needs to make a profit in order to thrive and continue.

finance know-how

It also needs to make money to beat the competition – it's the means of playing the game. You should only play this game if you can win, or at least win often enough to make it worthwhile.

From that, of course, other things will hopefully follow, as parts of the bigger picture of the success of that business – how it impacts on the world around it, how it looks after its employees, how ethical its production methods are or whatever. But if it is not a charity or a hobby, the money counts first and foremost. If you work for someone else, you must be paid your worth. If you're not getting paid, you're a volunteer (or an optimist at best, a fool at worst).

So while we are soulful about most areas of our lives and how we run this business, about this one thing we are not: in order to survive, notonthehighstreet.com *has* to make money. As we stand right now, our business is a classified success because it makes money. It makes money for thousands of people who run their own businesses and sell with us. It makes money to pay for our employees, for our investors and shareholders and for itself (that is, our net profit, to reinvest or put aside for when the company needs it). And yes, it makes money for the two of us.

We can honestly say that the last one – making money for ourselves – was the last thing on our minds when we started out. Not because we didn't want to make money, of course we did, and we'll freely admit we like the idea of never having to worry about money again. Indeed, we were determined to make money for our families but it wasn't the focus when we started the company. Still isn't. Instead, we instinctively knew that if we did the rest, our rewards would follow. We knew we each needed to be paid a basic, fair salary in order to keep doing the job but that was as much to ensure we were kept where we believed we needed to be – working for notonthehighstreet.com. Our sense of purpose came from building a business that was good for everyone and that would bring riches (not being soulful just yet, we still mean actual money) for everyone.

First off, then, we implore you to think of what you do as a business above all else; an enterprise that makes money. A business that you invest in, that has stakeholders, the power to enable others to thrive too, a plan and a future.

Holly: 'It's about how to sell yourself up, to move from thinking "Can I survive?" to "How do I make a million/double my turnover/make something I can truly call a business?" I don't find big numbers hard but sometimes I struggled to ground the number and make it reality. I need to feel that the aim is not completely crazy – though a little crazy is good – and I have a few ways of doing this. Looking at competitors both large and small helps you create a target. Maybe a business you admire or even one that has annoyed you, look at what they've done and then aim higher. Nothing beats competition as a motivator.

'It also helps to find out what makes the bank manager, investor or trade press tick when it comes to your industry. Listen to them and draw targets from their conclusions.

'It also could be based around the salary you want to draw. If you want to be able to double the salary you are on now within two years, work your numbers around that (without damaging your business) and it will give your topline number. Hold your breath and dive in!'

THE BUSINESS: PLANNING

Financial planning – not the two sexiest words in the English language when heard separately, let alone together. But if you're going to enjoy big, sexy success, you need to do your financial planning. Cost out your staff or support network, ongoing training, premises or workspace – both home and office, long-term investments and financial goals. Think, too, about your own personal expenditure in terms of what you need to spend in order to work effectively. Include in this your salary and profit, to establish what your revenues need to reach in order for your work to be viable and successful in the long term.

Sophie: 'You have to start with your overall goal. That's a little bit "dare to dream" but mostly a very practical, honest look at what your business needs to be – how big and how successful. At notonthehighstreet.com we knew the business had to be big in order to be successful – the spreadsheets told us that from the start. In that sense, I could be fearless. The other side – the passionate side, which is "I want this to be bigger than eBay because I know that it can be" – is about believing in the purpose.'

Our company is a small-margin one with a big outlay in technology, expertise and marketing. That's why we knew from the start that for it to exist it had to scale, hugely. That was obvious – there was no choice in the matter. To begin, we thought of some big – scarily big – numbers and then worked out how we were going to get there. But you might be able to get away with being smaller at first. Your business might turn a comfortable profit that serves you well without the pressure of driving for fast growth. What then? How do you make the decision if you have that choice, between shooting for the stars and enjoying a more lifestyle-oriented business? First we would ask if you are really sure. When you've done the sums and thought about what you need for your business, and your life, are you still absolutely sure that you can be modest? If you do feel that scaling up is a matter of choice, but you want that, where do the big numbers come from? That's where the conquer-the-world mentality comes in.

DAY 15 PRACTICAL EXERCISE: SET OUT YOUR FINANCIAL END GOAL
allow: two hours

Begin by identifying what you need to earn or what the business needs to make together with the costs involved, then work backwards from that. Your figures can be very rough at this stage – we'll get more precise later.

Once you've got your end goal in mind, you need to write some plans. We tended to start on the back of an envelope: roughly, we'd say that if we have to make a profit in two years' time, breaking even in a year's time, then what do our numbers need to look like in eighteen, twelve, six, three and one month's time? As with a set of balancing scales, you need to get a picture in your mind of what the revenue and costs might look like. At this stage, you can get comfortable with your initial financial targets. This applies to a career as much as to a business – taking time out to do an MBA, for example, is a big investment of time and money.

From there, you can get it down more formally and carefully on a spreadsheet. Play about with those initial numbers until they start to stack up and make sense, both the ins and the outs, what you'll make and what you'll spend, so that you can commit to them. You'll do it in even more detail in the financial forecasting below, but for now, focus on getting comfortable with the headline numbers.

PRACTICAL TIP

As a business owner, get an accountant if you haven't got one already. You need someone trustworthy and experienced who can give you guidance on everything from your projections to the labyrinthine systems of VAT and income tax. For accountants and financial advisors, be selective and don't get one you can't afford. Most of all, get one you trust absolutely and with whom you feel comfortable asking questions.

DAYS 16 TO 17 PRACTICAL EXERCISE:
FINANCIAL FORECASTING
allow: one and a half days

Put away the tarot cards and crystal ball. This is about putting together a set of spreadsheets that will constitute your two-year plan. For this, you need a 24-month profit and loss forecast (P&L) and a 24-month cash-flow forecast. The two are intrinsically linked as they are about the same information looked at in different ways. P&L is about your profitability whereas cash flow is about whether you're going to have enough cash in the bank at any one time to get there. Your accountant should be able to help you with this two-year plan.

Let's break down the work involved.

* **Establish your costs.** Note down every penny that has to be paid out to ensure you go to work, meet your objectives or make the product you sell. Include absolutely everything you can think of from train fares to postage, materials and office heating. Divide these figures into set-up costs (paid for once – e.g. equipment, branded stationery), production overheads (rent, utilities, salaries, membership subscriptions) and marketing costs.
* **Establish your revenues.** This is also called your topline income – the money coming through the door when you work or sell your product.
* **The P&L forecast.** Now you can sum up the revenues, costs and expenses incurred over a specific period of time, shown on

a monthly basis. Once you have this in hand, you'll be able to demonstrate your company's ability to generate more profit by a sales increase and/or reducing costs. Your spreadsheet should organise the data in rows of: sales income figures (be conservative here); direct costs (those directly related to a sale – raw materials, postage – if the cost changes according to the number of sales you make, then it's a direct cost); overhead costs (things you pay regardless of sales – salaries, rent, storage and so on); capital costs (these are incurred upfront but because you get the benefit over a longer period of time you can usually allocate them evenly over two to three years in your P&L to reflect that benefit). This spreadsheet should also show the totals before and after tax. The P&L total after tax is your most important figure: it's your net profit. That's what you can either take as bonus income for you or reinvest back into the business.

✳ **The cash-flow forecast.** Cash is king. This forecast will show you timing, allowing you to see instantly how much money you will have at any given moment. Once you've done your P&L, the 24-month cash-flow forecast will translate it into a statement of money coming in and costs going out, taking into account the timing of receipts and payments. It also means you can see ahead of time when you may need to borrow money or raise investment capital to tide you over those times when money has to go out but won't be coming in. If that happens, this makes it clear to you how much you will need to raise or fund to get you to a cash-positive position, as according to your two-year plan. For this new spreadsheet, have one section, 'Cash In', with three sub-headings to spread across the months: investment, loans, sales. In the next section, 'Cash Out', you'll write in: direct costs; overhead costs; capital costs; loan repayments; VAT and tax on profit; set-up costs. Your bottom line on this spreadsheet will show the cash coming in minus the cash going out. If it's in credit, that's money for reinvestment, to pay back loans and so on. If it's negative, then you have the clear picture you need to find new sources of cash or even revise your business model. With seasonal business, it will allow you to see when any negative cash position may occur and send up a red flag so that you can negotiate, say, a short-term solution such as an overdraft, to tide you over. The main difference between cash flow and P&L is timing. You should be able to show the impact of: a) credit given to customers over what time period; b) credit given by suppliers over what time period; and c) stock needs and cash required to make products and hold them.

Beyond this exercise, make sure you always keep good records so that you know how profitable you are. Keep checking your actual figures against your forecast and cash flow. You'll soon see whether you predicted accurately or wildly. It's a discipline you must have – don't wait for your accountant to tell you at the end of the year that you made a loss or for your bank to fine you for an exceeded overdraft.

DASHBOARD

Financial dashboards are a development of the KPI summary we talked about in Where Are You And Your Business Going? and are something every entrepreneur should refer to. For our suggested list of some of the likely indicators of the overall health of a business, see our dashboard checklist on page 271.

FUNDING

Once you've done your plan, you'll know how much it's going to cost you to get to where you want to go. Hopefully you're some of the way there – your own business is up and running, or your company is fully behind the initiative you plan to lead. You could be in the right job from which to springboard your career but you may have decided to make the leap. So whether your plans are to expand the business or take time off to retrain, you may need to work out how to fund the next level. The funding options below are relevant to start-ups but also to any business as it grows – eight years in we're still going out for new investment from time to time.

Grants

There's been a bit of shouting about government finance, so it's worth hunting for a grant. Many are time-consuming and difficult to win but the upside is they don't have to be repaid, so are well worth the effort. There have also been various government schemes to encourage small businesses, such as the GrowthAccelerator programme and Funding for Lending Scheme. Watch the press for the latest schemes as they change frequently.

Bank loans

The advantage of a bank loan is that it doesn't require you to give away any of your equity. The disadvantage is that most bank loans today are secured, which means your assets (house, usually) are risked against the loan. We wouldn't recommend this as too many businesses or plans fail for reasons beyond anyone's control.

DEALING WITH THE BANKS

In recent years, we've all had to deal with the fact that we're trying to grow businesses and scale up careers during a recession. It's undoubtedly made a hard job harder. Talking to some of our partners – small businesses and start-ups – made us realise just how difficult it's been. Yet, you can also take heart – they're all still here, they have managed to do more than just keep going, they have kept on growing. It seems that luck, timing and personalities all play their part (just as in the good times). The founder of My 1st Years says: 'Dealing with the banks during the recession was very difficult but the right bank manager is imperative. We had expected it to be a lot easier to deal with them.'

Pearl and Earl were less poetic: 'They were useless. Still are.' This partner made the good point that banks deal with all small businesses as a single group, and a small business is 'up to £50 million turnover', which does seem rather a large bracket.

Others have found it better than they expected. The founder of Ellie Ellie was a first-time business owner and was nervous. 'But none of it was scary in reality. In fact I have learned a lot from them and they have provided the business with exactly what it needed. We have now had two small-business loans from the bank in order to help us maximise sales over the Christmas period.'

When a business is doing well it probably helps with a positive interaction, too, as Sophia Victoria Joy says: 'As a small business we haven't experienced any difficulty during this time with the banks, we were always aware of the recession but have experienced only growth since the beginning.'

Venture capital and angel investment

Venture capitalists always want big growth and a major commitment but you probably do too, right? It's hard work to win VC finance and you will have to give away equity but the end result will be a serious investment in your company. Angel investors invest in a similar way, but are private individuals investing smaller sums, which suits early-stage and smaller businesses better.

Friends and family

Obviously risky, not least because those who love you may be tempted to lend you more than they can really afford and if everything goes wrong, it could be catastrophic for everyone involved, financially and emotionally. If you do go down this route, have a clear agreement as to how much is being lent as well as when and how it will be repaid.

Credit cards

We've done surveys at notonthehighstreet.com that have found that women will often back their business with a credit card and that they'd rather do that than find a grant or go to a VC. For obvious reasons, it's ill-advised to put yourself at risk of having to repay a credit card with high interest rates when all ventures are vulnerable to breaking down.

PROFITABLY PRODUCTIVE

Even if your company is not yet turning over a profit, you may well be on a 'path to profit' – in other words, there is a plan to show that if X, Y and Z are done, there will be a profit at the end. The path to profit is just as important, if not a tad more so, than the profit itself. There may be penny-pinching or even losses to cover until your business reaches a profit but in the meantime you're building valuable relationships, training staff and so on.

Holly: 'Sometimes I check in with the partners to see how they're doing if they're struggling to make money. Their margins can sometimes be so tiny that an extra five pence on postage is all it takes to push them into a loss-making situation. There are three possible things going wrong here: one, they're not charging enough for their products; two, they're spending too much on supplies and labour; three, they need to change the product altogether. What would make it worth more? Or cheaper to produce? Or do they need to muster the courage to scrap it altogether and say, "This one isn't for us"? Remember you're playing to win. Don't get too attached to your products or the service you're selling. Be ruthless.'

PAYING OTHER PEOPLE

There are things to think about when deciding what to offer a new employee. First of all, do make sure you address salary expectations as part of the interview process. In addition to salary, employees will value other things such as flexible working, the opportunity of equity or a one-off bonus. We offer a company bonus scheme, closely related to our annual performance – so that sales tracker we described in the chapter Where Are You And Your Business Going? shows our staff how close they are to achieving their bonus and at what level. That's motivating, engaging and something they can relate to and influence.

Before you hire anyone work out what you can afford, factoring in the total cost of hiring someone including NI and tax as well as providing a workspace and any equipment they may need. Consider the industry going rate – this will be determined by a number of things, from location to the scarcity or not of the skill you are recruiting for and the number of people looking for work.

Think about benefits and factor in the cost – these could be anything from the mandatory ones, now that workplace pensions are required by law, to the ones you choose to offer like a subsidised bicycle (that's how we started) to private healthcare (we've recently moved on to this).

Holly: 'It's so important to remember that money isn't everything. Make the benefits fit the type of business you run. We have a team who put on events for our departments – whether it's a sweetie trolley coming round the office occasionally, a beautician coming in, running the book club, cinema nights … And we're looking into how we can do more when it comes to flexible working, home working, holiday time, less-ordinary scholarships and so on. We keep that conversation going all the time.'

YOU

With the financial figures down on the spreadsheet, it's time now to approach money in a slightly different way. This is where we would like to encourage you to think about your own dreams for cash in the bank – to make the leap from being grateful for survival to doubling your turnover.

Holly: 'Money was never the only driver of notonthehighstreet.com; in some ways, we were lucky because the mission of the company was the strongest motivator of all – to provide a platform for small businesses. But I will admit that money was something I strived for because I am openly a personality that can only thrive if I have options, and money gives you freedom of choice. With cash in the bank, I spend more and can buy funky garden furniture, learn to fly and build a school in Africa. It has brought colour and allowed me to choose a less ordinary life.'

MONEY IS THE BAROMETER OF SUCCESS

At certain points in your journey, money matters. What it does for the business and what it does for you. The key is to keep a balance between not allowing the promise of money to distract you from doing the right thing for your business and remaining motivated. One investor told us: 'We want you to live on baked beans, but not the own-brand type.' In other words, they needed us to remain savvy and financially careful but not be so Scrooge-like with any profit that we were completely demotivated. You need to keep the pot at the end of the rainbow.

More than that, and more seriously, when it comes to the business itself (which is, remember, completely different from the personal income you make, even if it's your own company), money is the barometer for your company. It's how you calculate whether you're doing things right or wrong. Think of the money the business is making as points on a scorecard; if there's cash, you're winning. Like they say: no one ever went bust with money in the bank. Breaking even is nice – even better if that's after you've paid yourself a salary – but to have a surfeit means more for your business than just the dough itself. It means you can invest in the future, aim even higher, take some risks and make long-term strategic investments in building your brand and your customer offering/promise that won't see an immediate return but will make your business better, stronger, more long-lasting and more loved ... in the long run.

NICE TO KNOW

In the midst of the recession, October 2012, there was a news story that employment in the UK was at its highest since records began in 1971, largely accounted for by private-sector growth, together with the fact that the previous year had seen a record number of companies created, 99.5 per cent of which were SMEs (small and medium-sized enterprises, with a turnover of less than £25 million), accounting for 49 per cent of 2011's total business turnover in the UK. If you've got a good idea, this should encourage you to go for it!

Holly: 'I feel that money is an enabler – without it, the company wouldn't be here, the partners wouldn't have been able to get up and running. It gives you the ability to choose and enables your choices – that is a great thing about it. The power of money generally worries me. But I focus on what I can do with it to build and create happiness. Notonthehighstreet.com was built on fair trading terms so that all the businesses could thrive.'

Sophie: 'Since my first day at work, aged nineteen, I can remember thinking how all-consuming it all was and feeling quite stopped in my tracks by the idea that I was going to have to do it – work – all the time, for a very long time. The glaring conclusion I drew was that I should aim to get as high up as I could, as fast as I could and make as much money as possible, because it would be just as hard, if not harder, if I didn't.

'Building notonthehighstreet.com was the same, only to scale. Everyone in the office was working so flipping hard, our partners were working so hard, there was so much at stake, one thing was for sure – there needed to be a hell of a good by-product. Even if we loved every moment of it and knew we were doing something very worthwhile.

'Equally, there's no doubting that money is power. Make no mistake, if you're making money, or at least not losing money, you are more trusted to do things the way you believe they should be done. You get to make more of your own decisions. The flipside is obvious – if you're failing, you are more closely watched. You can become a foot soldier, following someone else's idea of what is right. I never wanted to be that person – my schooldays gave me more of that than I could wish for! Part of the reason I overdeliver is to ensure I keep my freedom as much as my money.'

BELIEVING IN YOUR VALUE

We're not encouraging anybody to pretend to be anything they're not
but we do want you to recognise your market value and not undersell
yourself. Money is globally understood and it means so much more than
numbers on a bank statement: that you and your worth are recognised by
your employers/backers/bank manager; or you stood up to someone who
might happily have seen you put down; or you've built a real business that
employs people and contributes to the economy; or you've graduated from
your kitchen table to a studio, or from your studio to an office; or you did
something that other people can't and did it well. There are other ways of
saying these things but money says it fast. And enjoyably. You can't deny
that. Some people still ask us, even now that we have cumulatively turned
over £200 million and employ about 200 people, 'Do you work full-time?
Do you have anyone to help you?' and the long answer, because you have
to put these people in their place for making assumptions (they don't ask
this question of men, we notice), is to describe the business, the number
of customers we have, how long since we started, the office we work in,
mumbling humbly about the home office potentially being a bit crowded
given the number of people we employ ... But the short answer, we're
sorry to say, is to look well paid and successful. That puts a sharp stop to
patronising questions.

When it comes to working out what you should be paying yourself or
charging as a fee for clients, don't stick a finger in the air and hope for the
best. Treat it as you would pricing a product. Do a little research and find
out what the market rates are. Then look at your own costs and think about
the profit you need to make. If you are thinking about a freelance rate, bear
in mind your market value too – factor in your experience, past successes

and so on. You should come up with a pricing formula that indicates your hourly rate and annual salary. With all this information in mind, you will find it much easier to quote a fee, salary or price to a potential client, boss or customer.

THE LANGUAGE OF MONEY

We recommend that you work on bringing the language of money inside your comfort zone. The bigger and older notonthehighstreet.com gets, the more everyday talk is of EBITDA, share class and cumulative ROI. Yes, it's technical but it's also what these things are. It's not pretentious or affected to use the right words so long as it's in the right context – it ensures that we all know what each other is talking about without lengthy explanation. That's why we need to know the language, understand it and use it. You need it in order to play the game and hold your own – it will give you confidence, it will empower you in the boardroom. It also shows courtesy and respect to your financial colleagues. This is why we make the effort, even though it is not our first love. That said, we always avoid using technical jargon in the wrong environment, where it can be construed as power play or one-upmanship. That's not our bag at all.

Holly: 'What I have realised is that when it comes to talking to the money people they are still of a certain ilk – highly educated and well-versed in their field. What you have to do is find the common ground so that personalities are not dampened in the board meetings. I learned the language of money in the same way that Harry learns his numbers in French. You have to do this quite literally – learn it, do a spelling test, understand it and use it. The way that you win a money conversation is by not losing yourself to it. I know that people have found it refreshing because I could converse with them in their language, but I also got them excited. If they said something I didn't understand, I'd ask them to put it in English and they'd have a chuckle. Or I'd even tell them that something was a load of old rubbish if they were being obtuse. It makes them laugh and puts us all on the same page again. But that approach and attitude only works because I have made the effort to learn the lingo.'

DAY 18 PRACTICAL EXERCISE:
LEARN THE LANGUAGE OF MONEY
allow: two hours

Just as Holly does, we'd like you to take time out to look up the financial terms and their meanings that surround your area of business. Make sure you are completely comfortable and ask lots of questions if something isn't crystal clear. It might be that you ask someone who is good with numbers or accounting to help you. But you should know, and be able to use with confidence, financial terms as well as understanding their implication, whether it's 'top line revenues' or 'gross margin'. The numbers of your own business should trip off your tongue just as easily – it shows you are master of your finances and that means anyone who invests in you will trust that you know what you are doing.

WE ASKED OUR PARTNERS

Did you need to raise capital? How did you do it?
Was it difficult? What were the challenges and
how did you overcome them? Do you fear money?

My 1st Years: Yes, we needed to raise capital. In fact I believe with a growing company there will always be a need to raise capital to get to the next stage of growth. We started cold-calling investors and eventually came into a bit of luck when we were introduced to our investor and he has been excellent for us. It is always difficult telling people to part ways with their hard-earned cash for a business that they know nothing about. The challenges were proving the potential and showing that my partner and I were very investable despite being young and inexperienced.

Highland Angel: I started my business with a personal loan, so didn't have to deal with the banks for finance. At the start I didn't pay myself anything at all, so in a way I was financing the business by working for nothing.

Ellie Ellie: I started Ellie Ellie in 2010 with no money at all, just a handful of jewellery findings, some old games from a charity shop, a camera and the internet. At that stage I had no assets behind me, nor a very good credit rating, having only just graduated. I wouldn't have been able to get any capital even if I tried! Once I started selling I would then reinvest the profits immediately and it's this strategy I still use today. We only reinvest once we have made the money; if we don't have the money we wait until we do, or we work out another way to do it. This doesn't mean we ever compromise or have to put things on hold until we get the money, because we don't. It just means we are making sure we can walk before we run. It also keeps our business creative by always thinking outside the box. I don't think I fear money, but I am cautious – I think every businessperson is or certainly should be. You have to be when you are dealing with real money and real people, it's a real-life game of Monopoly so be cautious both of running out of money and of knowing when and what to do with it. Having grown Ellie Ellie from no money whatsoever to the company it is today gives me confidence to trust my entrepreneurial instinct and the power of money, without fear.

Pearl and Earl: We started with my personal overdraft. Since then we have raised some money with grants but that's all. The business is our only family income so we have to make it work. Luck, judgement and juggling were skills at the beginning and are just as valuable now. Cash flow is everything when you are small. I only fear money when I don't have any.

Sophia Victoria Joy: I initially started out with the last £200 of my student loan, slowly building up from there. It wasn't a large sum of money, but I was ready to begin something special and put it to good use. To begin with it was very difficult. As a graduate supporting myself financially it was a struggle. I knew that if I stuck with it and kept my focus I would make it work – belief in my ability saw me through. I am not afraid of money. As we have grown I am more confident in the choices I make with money and seeing this succeed time and time again instils further confidence in myself.

The customer, the customer – so important we had to say it twice

'People don't care how much you know until they know how much you care.'

JOHN C. MAXWELL

DAYS 19 TO 22

Knowing who your customer is and how to
connect with them; improving customer service;
a guide to marketing channels.

We've said it before and we'll say it again. The customer lies at the very heart of any business. Not the product, service, price point, brand or location or even you. All of these matter, of course, but the starting point, the thing that informs everything else is the customer. Who are you selling to, are you talking to them and are they listening?

For us, it was easy – we knew we liked our customers (and still do) as much as anything else. In that sense, it always boiled down to a one-to-one relationship like any other. But in scale. For people to like you it isn't right to give them something for nothing; nor should you grovel for their approval. It's the same with customers – you must create a relationship of mutual respect. We have something they value and we try to offer it with charm, honesty, dignity and a sense of our own worth. At the same time, we show humility and gratitude for their custom. This happens quite naturally because we like them. We find them clever and amusing – in the products they choose and how they customise them, for instance – and touching, in the stories they tell us about why they're choosing, buying or giving a certain thing. We mean this without any cynicism; we believe that this mutual respect is central to a successful relationship with a customer. You do, of course, have to scale it and find a way to talk on a

your customer

mass level to hundreds of thousands of people at once, without making them feel like a number. So we work very hard, for instance, at keeping our emails genuinely relevant and meaningful and are careful about to whom they are sent. Because if you were sent only irrelevant round-robin emails from someone you'd thought of as a friend, you'd consider being a bit unavailable the next time they asked to meet up for a cup of coffee, wouldn't you? It's as uncomplicated as that, only with some extraordinary technology now able to help you.

While your customer may not necessarily be an end-consumer but another business, a financier or an individual, we are going to make a distinction for the sake of the book. This chapter will focus on the retail consumer, that is, the buyer of a product or service to whom you are directly selling. In the next chapter, we'll talk about customers in the broader definition that they can also be the business you work for, an agency or clients. (The next chapter also talks about PR, which is another way of talking to customers, a marketing channel in itself.) There are lessons to be learned in both chapters that can be applied across the board and the lines do blur but here we mainly have the end-consumer in mind when we say we want to talk about knowing your customer and connecting with your customer.

However you define your customer, they're always people and you need to know their motivations. Before you can progress in your business, you need to know them inside out – what they need, their expectations from you/your product, who else they might buy from/hire instead and whether you are able to look after them properly should anything go wrong.

Knowing your customer typically comes from two kinds of information: first, personal insight, based on qualitative research, which might mean meeting several of them in a room and hearing what they have to say about your brand, or doing other open-ended research that gives you insight into their motivations and behaviours. That also allows you to create vivid images and descriptions of them (sometimes called personas) that you can refer to later when it comes to making any decisions about marketing or communications. This is coupled with the second kind, based on the analysis of data – statistical information about your customer, the quantitative side of knowing them.

Connecting with your customer, when we talk about it here, means marketing to them on the basis of understanding them and making it a two-way conversation. And we believe that connection is at its strongest when it draws on the principles of empathy, creating an emotive bond between your brand and the person you're selling to. So while we strongly advise you to master the practical skills – which include marketing channels and the technology of connecting with customers – we also urge you always to remember that marketing is about finding, then growing, that relationship at the most human level. In short, Twitter is not about the platform or the technology, it's about the conversation that it fuels; successful SEO (search engine optimisation) is not a dark art, it's about demonstrating your relevance and importance to your customer (only via a robot) and signposting your brand. At the heart of that connection is your brand itself, that is, the principles of your customer offering and your business that are most meaningful to your customers.

Although customers are human and therefore messy, emotional and unpredictable – and you need to be flexible enough to respond to that – there are structured approaches that will help you to manage them. This is where relevant marketing channels and customer service come in, in conjunction with CRM (customer relationship management).

Knowing your customer and connecting with your customer are two different things and yet they achieve the same thing: a good, strong business with your customer at the heart of it. Ultimately, this means sales and profits.

FIRST, *KNOW* YOUR CUSTOMER . . .

The aim in knowing your customer is to be in a position to provide a consistent, inspiring and brand-defining experience when you set out to connect with them throughout every interaction they have with the business. Whether they are browsing your website, following you on Twitter, choosing a product, or receiving confirmation of an order, every time any of these things happens they are exposed to your brand. Your message and style of communication must be consistent at every stage to have the greatest effect. Putting it simply: to know them well is to be able to connect with them well and to be in the best possible position to give people a reason to come and do business with you.

You may feel you already know your customer pretty thoroughly. But by refreshing your research and constantly asking questions you will optimise your existing opportunities and find game-changing new ones. If you want to step your business up a level – whether that's growth, expanding your product lines or changing your price points – knowing your customer will enable you to do these things coherently.

INSIGHT AND CUSTOMER PROFILING

So, how can you get to know your customer better?

To get marketing right (we come to the specific tools, channels and methods later in the chapter) you first need to work out what goes on in your customer's mind. This is done by knowing your customer in a 3-D way and having that at the heart of everything you do. Humans process information in two ways: first, by systemising (looking at how things work; thinking about how to control the system); and secondly, by empathising (connecting appropriately and predicting behaviour). Broadly speaking, men tend towards systematic approaches, which appeal to the rational, logical part of the brain; and women, empathetic, drawing on the emotional, instinctive part.

Women form the majority of our customer base, so we try to reflect the empathetic decision-making process. One of the ways in which we do this is by getting to know specific individual customers at the deepest possible level. When we set out to create personas, we avoided the typical approach, because everything about our brand and all its uniqueness tells us we don't have a typical customer. The traditional method is that a marketing team might create a cardboard cutout of a single imagined customer and attribute to that a fictional character, together with certain behaviours and desires. Instead, we did a major project to identify and learn everything we could about six real-life people who are especially representative of key groups of our customer base.

Using our databases, we were able to single out these six different real-life customers according to behaviours we already knew – those that spent a certain amount of money, a certain amount of times, on certain groups of products, say – and then actually find those people. We approached those individuals and with their explicit permission spent days in their company, learning about and understanding them, and made films of them for the whole company to see. We put together scrapbooks with information about their lives, backgrounds, preferences, inspirations, likes and dislikes, as well as about the way they shopped and what they looked for when buying generally, not just from notonthehighstreet.com. In this way, the whole company can really know the customer – if we are discussing a technological development, product ideas, pricing or PR, we are able to say, 'How would Lucy or Kate relate to this?'

Here's a snapshot of some of the things our identified customers said:

Kate: 'I live in a tiny village but in my twenties I was a radio producer and lived the high life in Notting Hill ... I'm hopeless at going to the cinema as I chat too much. I like a happy ending. I like all the Pixar movies – they make me cry ... I like spending time researching the right gifts for people. We all have so much unnecessary stuff these days and I guess if I'm going to give somebody something I want to spend time considering what will make them happy.'

Lucy: 'I'm a member of Tate Modern and I'm often to be found just sitting and staring at a piece of art ... I like things to tell stories or say something about me ... I really love to nail a present. It's a joyful thing to take them back to a shared memory. I like design-led things, not "crafty" things. I love knowing that things have been made by someone with a passion or a skill.'

Just by reading these fragments, you can see how we can share with the rest of the company the subtleties of real people's thought processes and the colour of their driving emotions far more effectively than we might with a generic statement such as 'Our customers like art and movies.' The beauty of it is that because these customers are at the statistical bull's eye of our business, the scientists can believe in it as much as those who respond more emotively.

DAYS 19 TO 20 PRACTICAL EXERCISE:
KNOW YOUR CUSTOMER
allow: bite-sized periods of time over two days

This is a short version of something you could spend longer on another time. But, for now, these exercises will help you get to know your customer even better. You don't need to spend too long – just thirty minutes on each task below will get you results that should surprise and interest you. You need to be completely open to finding out exactly who your customer is and that means the answers are going to be found on the shop floor.

✴ Watch your target customer in action – go out and observe them in competitor shops or read forums on competitor websites, for example. Look at how they behave, what items they choose, what they put back on the shelf.
✴ Phone three people you trust and ask for their honest opinion about something such as your logo or key product offering.

✳ Do a fast online poll – set up a quick vote with the outline of a product idea and ask a single question, such as 'Should we or shouldn't we launch this?' Or, 'Do you like this idea?' (Don't say too much, so that you can be sure that your ideas are safe even before you take care of your copy or design rights. Find out more about how to protect your ideas through resources listed in The Directory.) You can tweet the survey link and put it on the end of your emails (in your signature strip) then go back to it in a few days to see what it tells you. This is an example of what the founders of what became Innocent did, although theirs was face-to-face rather than online, when they set up a stall at a festival and asked people whether they should give up their jobs to make smoothies. They asked people to throw their empty bottles into a 'yes' or 'no' bin.

✳ Ask three people if you can watch them shop online, to see how they use websites.

✳ If you have a customer service department, man the phones yourself and keep a tally of the kind of questions that are being asked or problems that occur.

None of these things are statistically sound research but done at any time they will keep you connected to your customers and keep you thinking about what it is your customers want. You need to keep your own ears to the ground and not always rely on others to report back to you.

Alongside these results, analyse your sales and product data, which you should always have up to date and to hand, and from all of this you should be able to draw up tribes or typical customer groups. This will help you answer these critical questions:

* Who is your core customer? How do you know?
* Where do they shop? What do they buy?
* What motivates your customer?
* How much do they spend on different things?
* Can you expand your customer base?

Review your competitors:

* How are other businesses targeting your customer?
* Do you think they're successful?
* What are the measures of their success?
* Is there anyone offering a similar product/service/job as you?

... THEN *CONNECT* WITH YOUR CUSTOMER

Once you truly know your customer, the battle is 90 per cent won. Back to the friendship analogy: if you know, for example, that your friend falls for flattery above all else, then the way to get her to do something for you is to tell her nobody does it better. It's the same with customers: if you know what they value, then asking them to buy, do or respond to something is simple.

In some ways, our job is made easier by the fact that notonthehighstreet.com offers so many personalised items – it's a direct route to our customers' emotional touchpoints. We're both fans of the team at Pretty Little Head, marketing specialists who have done much work to develop and communicate an understanding of the two key ways in which our brains respond to marketing (as on page 176). They've shown that even apparently systematic brands can seek an emotional connection with their audience. Google, for example, changes its logo regularly and this seemingly small detail is what demonstrates that people are behind the site. Of course, there are those that want to appeal to the systematic customers – car marketing, for example, will focus on performance and statistics.

A strong empathetic approach is to mirror your audience, to provide a brand that makes them feel 'That's for people like me.' It creates a feeling of mutual appreciation and recognition. We would also recommend that you look to convey a sense of the people behind the brand – it's humanising in a cyber world. When you do this, speak as your customers speak; you can do this through reference to subject matter they know (people, feelings, cultural references), social currency (jokes, anecdotes, gossip), patterns (a depth of detail), form (headlines, bullet points), a subtextual dynamic (sharing, to build a closeness). Finally, try as much as you can to focus on the sensory and the subtextual, those 'between the lines' notions that can really trigger your customers' touchpoints.

DAY 21 PRACTICAL EXERCISE:
DEFINE YOUR CUSTOMER EXPERIENCE
allow: one hour

Now you know your customers a little better, consider what it is about your customer offering, and the experience it delivers, that seals the deal for your customers. The key pillars of our customer experience are:

✳ Curation of original and inspiring products (with a close eye on quality and range).
✳ Personalisation/customisation of many products (being innovative).
✳ Simple, pleasurable experience you can trust (being personal and inspiring).

All of these things are underpinned by our brand promise, a life less ordinary, which equals a distinctive customer-focused offering, and we make sure that they are the basis of every single touchpoint we exchange with our customers.

To find your key pillars, take a simple approach based on your own instincts about your business. Write down ten things you think are important and distinctive about your offering and how they interact with your customers. Ask some customers if they agree and reduce that list of ten to three or five. The aim here is to come up with universal truths about your business, the core pillars – not details. Test them, play with them, be honest with yourself about them. Do they really ring true? Can you deliver on them? Are they the most relevant?

TECHNOLOGY

Technology has turned the customer experience inside out, and the change isn't over yet. Can you remember what a 'retail experience' was twenty or so years ago? A battle down the high street on a Saturday morning. We all did it and we all accepted that it meant badly lit, squashed changing rooms, queues that snaked for miles (each customer writing out a cheque – remember how *long* that took?) and, to top it all, bored, gum-chewing shop assistants.

Now we want fireworks when we go shopping and nothing less will do. High-street shops are 'worlds' with softly lit 'transformation spaces', contactless payment and helpful 'personal stylists'. Yet even this is medieval when compared to online shopping. When it comes to finding a way to shop that is fresh and new, the internet has got the edge. Even established brands such as M&S are finding that their customers are turning to the new-fangled world wide web, with over a third of their dresses and one in five suits sold online. At notonthehighstreet.com we've seen consistent explosive growth every year, even during one of the most difficult periods of retail trading in recent decades.

All of which is to say that customers in the twenty-first century routinely expect innovation. They are exploring new ways of sating their desires and prefer those places that can keep up the pace. For you or your business, you need to look at what developments are available for you to adopt and see if you can apply them for your customers' benefit. Our marketplace format at notonthehighstreet.com is successful because it is able to be experimental, exciting, new and in tune with consumer trends without excessive commercial risk. Other businesses might throw out a novel product or new pricing system, trying it out just to see how their consumers respond. This is more easily done if your company is based online or is small in scale as there won't be any great cost.

CRM: CONNECTING *AND* KNOWING ...

There's one area of customer communication that is a constantly self-fulfilling cycle of knowing and connecting, endlessly communicating and improving the message and its delivery, based on what's learned at every cycle: customer relationship management (CRM). It's all about making sure the communications you send your customers, whether online or offline, are targeted and relevant. We have around 2 million people that we are able to send marketing communications to, so we have to be sure that we are contacting them in the right way. As a first step, we were able to define twenty-eight different customer segments, based on how often they bought from us, what they bought and how much they spent. This meant, for example, that we could then be sure that an email highlighting a product that costs £50 is not sent to a customer that spends, on average, less than £20 a time with us.

The number one principle we follow is relevance and this isn't only about expenditure but also about a customer's browsing behaviour. As a company grows and scales up, you have to work to keep the communications right for your customers or they can mentally – if not actually – unsubscribe. Sending out the same email to your entire database every Monday morning is eventually going to fail. Our technology allows us to see whether emails have been deleted or read and to respond accordingly, so we are constantly analysing responses and readjusting the emails we send out. Analyse your customers as far as you can, looking at who buys what, when and how much they spend and then tweak your communications as necessary. You can then track which emails are performing; if one isn't, try another. If a customer doesn't click on three emails about home goods, for example, we will send her a communication from a different – but still relevant – segment. The glory of e-communications is that they're all measurable, trackable and relatively simple to do, especially with some of the tools we suggest in The Directory. Use them to your advantage.

BRAND UNDERSTANDING

Your brand is at the heart of how you connect with your customer – some of this will play forward into the next chapter, with you at the core of your brand.

'Brand' is a small word with a big meaning. But at its core is how your customers perceive you – and that is something you can control in a number of ways, from what you offer and how you behave to your logo and the content on your website to packaging, the magazines you advertise in and even how you style your invoices. While all of these things encapsulate your brand, none of them in isolation are your brand itself. Any brand is made up of many, many interdependent elements, like the twigs in a bird's nest. When shaping your brand, you will have identified key principles that make your brand what it is. At notonthehighstreet.com, for example, ours are: to be always relevant, personal, creative, inspiring, collaborative and original. Everything we do, whether serving our customers or deciding what to put in our reception area, is guided by these principles and if we stick with them, we can be sure that we are delivering on our promise, our end line, 'choose a life less ordinary'.

But every brand evolves and you need to ensure that you are still reflecting back the things you have learned to the guiding principles. We have always been very clear about our brand but evolution can present new challenges. For us, the question of how much 'being British' matters to our brand comes up over and over again as we look to international growth.

Branding is the term used to describe your visual identity, encompassing your logo, trademark, design, fonts, signature colours and slogan (or strapline) if you have one, which will appear on everything from your website to your marketing material and your company stationery. All of these things carry a message – one you can see even in the very pages of this book, we hope – and it's important that you ask yourself what exactly it is that you want to communicate to your customers about your business. Funky and original? Traditional and sage? Minimalistic and understated? In a world where technology is developing at breakneck speed, better design will win the race. Spend time and money getting your brand identity right – you'll be living with it for a very long time.

Finally, when you have pulled together your brand principles, branding and customer knowledge, you can start to be very effective in your marketing. At this point, deciding how to communicate with your customers and what exactly you want to communicate come into play and you can and should be thinking about what will be certain to make the customer buy, either directly or indirectly. We'll get into this detail now – just one word of caution: watch out for brand dilution. When you first launch – or relaunch – you'll find it hard to resist the quick-buck temptations, the one-stop shops that promise an instant fix, whether it's blanket discounts to ensure that one-click sale or buying vast customer lists and emailing everyone on it several times a week. They are nothing more than cheap tactics and while we've been tempted in the past, we have always come to realise that they would have only served to undermine our brand principles.

THE TOOLS AND CHANNELS OF CONNECTION

We believe that the most powerful way to sell something is to sell it with emotion. This might sound like a big ask, not to mention close to impossible when it comes to your average cynical, wised-up consumer, resistant to the manipulative tricks of retailers with their mood music and wafts of freshly baked bread aromas. But you can do it at both micro and macro levels.

At a micro level, for example, we'll send emails targeted to groups of people that we know are interested in a certain thing. But at a macro level, we'll be looking for an overall message to communicate and we do that by finding the common ground between our customers, whether they live in a terraced house in Plymouth or a castle in Scotland. It may be that they have different amounts of money to spend but they're both looking for something that is thoughtful, original and different. When you find that common thread, the more emotional and soulful message becomes easier to find.

Brands such as Dove do this very well, as with their campaign for real beauty. Ultimately they're selling face creams and deodorant but they've done it by using positive role models and real women. It's a very soulful message and the polar opposite of L'Oréal's scientific approach (which also works but in a completely different way).

The tone of voice and insight that you employ in your message should also ensure that your customer's response is: 'Oh yes, I recognise that.' In this way, you can tap into the relationship that you are building with each other.

Don't worry if you think half or more of the channels below aren't for you or your business – think of it like a pick-and-mix stand, choose what works for you and leave the rest.

MARKETING CHANNELS

Marketing channels are the practical tools of selling your business and communicating your brand, both online and offline. Each one is useful in its own way but when it comes to moving your business on to the next level, certain channels will have better connectivity power than others. It's worth thinking about these carefully before devoting yourself to any – each channel needs planning, strategy and resource; you don't need all of them, all at once. For guidance, we've rated each channel's connectivity power – that is, how well it helps build strong, long-term, relationships with customers in a way that a business can control – on a scale of 1 to 5 (1 = strong; 5 = weak). You'll also find that where we mention online resources or digital tools, we've listed where to find them in The Directory.

(While we've got you here – just a quick note about PR. We talk about it in the next chapter – where it's particularly relevant in the context of talking about you at the core of your business – but we wouldn't want you to think that it shouldn't be handled with the same discipline as the rest of the channels, when it comes to budget, message, strategies and so on. PR is part of the mix, not something separate.)

On the web

Company website: Any business operating today, whether it's offering a transactional site or not, must plan its online strategy. Not only must a business be easily found by search engines but it needs to be at the centre of the right social media networks and it all revolves around the content you can develop as a business to reinforce your brand purpose and your relevance to your target audience. As an individual, you can control a great deal of your visible online presence and this could be significant when it comes to finding yourself a better job. It's not just about having a large contacts book on LinkedIn. You can, for example, demonstrate awareness of your wider industry through highlighting articles, retweeting interesting statistics and quotes or even writing a blog with your opinions about industry discussions that are taking place. Similarly, for your own business, customers can be encouraged to discuss your products or services, 'like' you on Facebook and so on. Being in the middle of these conversations means you are able to talk directly to your customers. But you must take a strategic approach to your online content as with any other area of your business.

Connectivity rating: 2

Email marketing: Email is a way of talking to both existing and prospective customers. It's important to grow your own subscriber list, rather than buying names. Emails must have engaging subject lines, while the content itself should have a clear call to action – a hyperlink to your website and a limited-edition product, for example. Using CRM technology you can tailor your emails beautifully to suit the recipients.

Connectivity rating: 4

Blog: Running your own blog is a low-cost way of bringing you and your business to life for your customers, whether you are talking about the day-to-day running of it, products you are developing or quotes and images that inspire you. Linking a blog to your website, as well as to your email signature and social media channels, will help grow the readership and will also benefit your search engine rankings. But you must be careful that you stay on message in your blogs – as they are personal, it's all too easy to go off-piste and risk diluting your brand message. Be sure to plan your content and make a commitment to regular posts, even if it's only once a month.

Connectivity rating: 3

Social media

Facebook and Twitter still dominate, but others like Pinterest, Instagram, Snapchat and Vine are storming the market, widening the definition of social media and growing constantly.

Facebook: A company Facebook page (as opposed to an individual account) is an engaging and informal way of talking to your customers. It's the online version of gathering all your best customers in a bar for a quick drink and chat. However, it won't work to your advantage unless you plan exactly how you're going to use it. To share news? Test ideas? Get to know more about your customers? Remember, too, that comments can be negative as well as positive. Monitor your wall frequently and be sure to address any negative issues so that everyone can see complaints are being dealt with, even if you take the conversation elsewhere to do so. It's very easy to set up a company Facebook page but the era of free social media is now over and for you to build an audience for the page and broaden the engagement around the content you post, you'll need to spend some of your marketing pounds on this and tracking tools.

Connectivity rating: 3

Twitter: **With its 140-character tweets, this social media phenomenon is** great for giving a very direct response to relevant events, demonstrating to followers that your business is tuned in and for finding prospective new customers. There are free tools available, like TweetStats, to help you find out who the key influencers are for existing Twitter users and your competitors. Use tools that tell you the best times to tweet, how often, who the top followers are, what tweets lost you followers, which gained you some and so on. Be careful to manage the attention you give Twitter and be mindful of RTs (retweets), which can spread rumours like wildfire. Consider your tweets carefully before posting them. Just like with Facebook, Twitter has a suite of advertising products that you can use to attract new audiences to your brand and to enable you to advertise around the big news topics on the social network.

Connectivity rating: 3

Advertising online

PPC (pay-per-click): **A search engine will quickly show you PPC ads –** they're the ones that appear in a separate box at the top of the search results or to the right-hand side. They can be bought by anyone who wishes their website to come up when certain key search words are entered. If you do this, either through Google AdWords or Bing, you will pay every time someone clicks on your ad. The amount paid is decided by a live online auction and each click can vary in cost from a few pence to over

£50, depending on the industry you are targeting and the keywords you want to bid on. You can control how much you'd like to bid and your total budget, so the cost will never be more than you can afford.

The most important thing here is that you track which key words are converting to sales. It's a great way to kick-start a small business, particularly if your website is not currently appearing high on the organic search-engine results. It can, however, be complicated to get this working well – you may spend your whole budget for no return. Use specialist agencies or learn as much as you can about how to target your customers and be prepared to spend money during the test phases. Remember every click you drive equals traffic to your website, bringing with it valuable potential earnings.

Connectivity rating: 5

Display advertising: The newer forms of display advertising – the broad term for any banner ads – include retargeting, which means a user is shown relevant ads for your company after they visited the site even if they didn't buy anything. If you look at a dress on a site, then go to read an online magazine, you'll probably see ads for that dress pop up. This can be a very effective way of targeting a customer and persuading them to return to your site to make a purchase. Avoid pay-per-view deals rather than pay-per-click, or you'll be paying even when users don't click back to your site.

Connectivity rating: 4

Affiliate marketing: This is when you reward other websites for delivering sales to your business by paying them a commission for every sale delivered. Websites do this by displaying your banners or content. There are a number of UK affiliate networks that can do this for you, managing the payment of commissions and reporting on your behalf. This model is cost-effective (you only pay per click or per sale made) but this isn't to say you mustn't keep a close eye on costs and negotiate the best terms possible. Watch out for monthly management costs and use only those sites that are complementary to your brand.

Connectivity rating: 5

Climbing the search engine ladder

SEO (search engine optimisation): **Google, Bing and Yahoo!** are all search engines. When any user types in keywords, they get two sets of results, 'paid', and 'organic' or 'natural'. Paid results are PPC. Organic results are those that the search engine has decided are relevant to your enquiry and SEO is the work that you do to help the search engine rank you highly. Exactly how they make this decision is based on a complicated series of algorithms that are constantly adjusted and never revealed. As a general rule, however, they will scan websites looking for these keywords though there is a whole host of other factors that determine where websites are ranked.

Websites recommended by others and social media shares can also boost your results. But take care – wallpapering your own website with the keywords can lead to dismissal by the search engine. It's skilled and in a highly competitive market it can take months if not years to reach the top spot. It's better that you work hard on getting your website absolutely right for your business and therefore recommended by your customers – eventually, that will improve your SEO with better results than any agency can guarantee and allow you to connect with your customers on a highly authentic basis.

Connectivity rating: 3

Offline

Direct mail: This is anything you send customers in the post, whether a catalogue or a postcard. It can contain a call to action – a discount or promotional code – which is easy to track and measure. Be careful to work within data protection laws if you use this method to capture data about people's names and addresses and always make it clear and easy for customers to unsubscribe. It's expensive but costs are negotiable – except for postage. The use of CRM here, too, will ensure that only those customers who are interested in your offering will receive information – it means you're not sending out 'junk mail', which both irritates prospective buyers and wastes your money.

Even as an online business, we use offline, more traditional marketing channels and catalogues have been the most important area of direct mail for us. The truth is, customers still enjoy the tangible sensation of having something in their hands, flicking the pages of a catalogue and tearing out their favourite products to pin on the fridge. When we launched our first catalogue the company had been up and running for two years, the cost was terrifying (it came to more than our entire first year's marketing budget), involved an enormous amount of extra work and there was a niggling fear that paper was dead. Our business was *online*, why were we sending out catalogues – surely so last century? But it worked.

Connectivity rating: 3

Radio advertising: All commercial radio stations sell advertising slots and sometimes make the ads for you too. You can localise according to region or timing (for example, a product for parents can be advertised during the school run). It's a tricky medium to measure unless you have a special offer or competition.

Connectivity rating: 3

Press advertising: Ads in newspapers and magazines are sold according to size and position – right-hand pages are more expensive than those on the left (notice how you flick through a magazine next time). You can also buy advertorials – ads designed to look as if they're editorial. Press ads are still very effective, particularly when it comes to brand alignment – a luxury clothes designer will advertise in *Vogue* as much for the association than as a driver to sales. Again, it's a harder one to measure unless you offer a discount or deal only available to readers.

Connectivity rating: 3

Television: Advertising on TV is probably the easiest way to reach a very large audience with your message but it does require a significant investment in both buying the advertising space and production of the ad itself. You choose your slot according to the audience – e.g. ABC1 adults – and, on certain channels, the slots can be bought regionally in order to test the impact of TV before you commit to a national campaign. You need to work with a media buying agency to ensure you get value for money for the spots you are buying but be aware this is not cheap and going on TV is not a step that should be taken lightly.

The effectiveness can be measured, but you need to understand what it is you're trying to do. If you're trying to drive awareness of your brand, you can run pre- and post-campaign tracking research to test shifts in awareness and perception. If you want to drive direct sales, you can measure the impact on turnover during the campaign but only if the TV advertising is not running at the same time as any other advertising. Any ad needs to be sent to Clearcast as a script and a final edit to make sure it complies with the TV Advertising Standards Code.

Connectivity rating: 3

CUSTOMER SERVICE

For us, there are two key elements when it comes to running our customer service department. One is to consistently define and deliver outstanding service to every customer; the other is to manage the customer service team so that we can be sure they are equipped to do that. As our company has grown, the customer service team has grown with it, from eight people three years ago to around forty today. This has created a challenge of its own; when you're small it's easy to provide good customer service but as you grow, how can you measure that consistency of quality? And when it comes to the team itself, we have had to focus more on leadership than management; we work to embed our cultural values with the team, connecting customer service to every area of the business.

We've all heard the expression 'The customer is always right' but in modern retail 'The customer always comes first' is more fitting. You might grow a better business, serve more customers well and have an improved reputation by showing confidence and authority when challenged, rather than always giving in against your better judgement. Just so long as you have your facts straight first – if the customer is right and you have made a mistake, then admit it, quickly, and correct it. But if they're not, be true to your policies and strategies. If these are good, the customer should be satisfied.

Core to our company is the importance of measuring and in customer service what is measured has changed enormously in the last few years. Good customer service is no longer rated by how long a call takes but on the impact on the customer – how satisfied are they? What is the impact on them of the phone call?

To help us achieve better measuring, we put ourselves forward for the top fifty customer service awards; these have given us goals to reach for. The awards are divided into five areas: timeliness, ease of use, reliability, knowledge and personalisation. The last pillar is about the tone, content, relationship and the individual – ironically, it's about the thing that doesn't get measured, as when a customer says, 'I can't really tell you why they were lovely, they just were.' The important thing about this pillar is that it leads to recommendations.

The personal touch is where we can really excel and that's in part because although we are big, our partners are small and each one of them is able to act as a small customer service agent, with one-on-one relationships with the customers. A customer once phoned us because her husband had died serving in Iraq and she wanted a bracelet delivered on the Saturday in time for the funeral on Monday. Our partner not only sent the personalised bracelet in time but felt moved to send flowers to the funeral.

As your company grows and gets bigger there will be a shift not only in your customer base but also in their expectations and you have to work hard to stay ahead of the trend. Technology has made a huge difference here; customers calling now may expect you to know just from their name what order they made and what stage it's at. If you don't have the technology to do this – it does cost a lot of money – you need to work at managing the customers' expectations and keeping them onside as you ask the necessary questions.

The flipside of our speciality – product personalisation – is that it is an emotional flashpoint for customers. When they buy something that is extra personal they've thought about all the things that could make a gift perfect for their friend or whomever they're buying it for, so they're investing more in it than just money. You have to keep this in mind because it means that, for them, when something goes wrong, it *really* goes wrong. (But when it goes right – wow!)

Where customer service can come into its own is when it means that customers are speaking to real people. As we've grown, we've moved away from templates, allowing all the reports to be written by the team members, and this has hugely increased our customer satisfaction. We also introduced postcards that staff or partners can send out after a customer has been in contact for whatever reason. The card might say 'Thank you' or 'Good luck' or even, when things very rarely go wrong, 'Sorry'. We send out about 5,000 cards in a year – most of them probably get put up on the fridge. That's a very positive message to put in our customers' houses.

DAY 22 PRACTICAL EXERCISE:
REVIEW YOUR CUSTOMER SERVICE
allow: three hours

✳ Look at the rules and practices for customer service that you first drew up for the business. Are they still relevant today? Do they reflect the evolutions in your brand? Is the language for greeting customers the right one?

✳ Check that any returns policy, returns address and company information on your website and paperwork is all in order.

* Check you are complying with the relevant legislation (see The Directory).

* Are you keeping to the time frame for dealing with a customer enquiry? If not, schedule time first thing in the morning and at the end of the day for this task. While you want to keep the conversation real with a customer, it's key too that you have a systematic approach. Leave a complaint too long and you could create a backlog of angry customers. The temptation then will be to give them the product for free just to rescue the situation.

* What does your customer really need from you? Is it a prompt email response or a personal phone call? Are you meeting those needs?

* What's your system for dealing with negative complaints? Is everyone in the company – not just the customer service team, if you have one – fully apprised of this? (Our best advice here: remove the emotion from the story and leave yourself with the certainties, which, whether around legal issues or otherwise, can be resolved while retaining the picture of the complaint. You don't want to get into an emotional quagmire if you can possibly help it. But always listen.)

WE ASKED OUR PARTNERS

How do you go about trying to understand your customers?
What interactions best help you?

My 1st Years: We have a VIP list of customers and my partner and I often speak to them and ask questions. We also get stuck in with customer service to find out what is currently going on within the business.

Oakdene Designs: My mother is right in the target market – she convinced me to become a seller in the first place. A lot of ideas will go through her first.

Ellie Ellie: Our independent feedback comes through a customer reviews service called Feefo and is also a great way to develop our products and services, as we take all feedback constructively and there's always room for improvement. All interaction with our customers is a great source of information for us to use and develop. Some of our best product developments, such as our unique proofing service on our map products to our engravings on our pendants, have all principally developed from customer feedback and interaction.

Maria Allen: I love hearing from my customers, whether they are giving feedback, asking about a new design or telling me the story behind their purchase. Often they will suggest things that will lead to us developing new products so I am grateful to hear from them.

Pearl and Earl: When we started it was about what I liked and I had an idea of who it was pitched to ... like-minded folk really. That initial view has not essentially changed and reviewing online data just gives us more details. We prefer to operate in the influencer category but as a business we need to communicate to more of them to drive our revenue. Our craft customers are super-loyal (80 per cent return) and our returning customers spend double what they did with their first order. My job is to find the products that they don't know they need yet. Shows and phone calls are always good to get some feedback and tools like Feefo and social networks are helpful too.

What's most important in delivering great customer service?

Bookishly: Being human. There has to be some process, but I still do all my own customer service and I want people to know that I am a real person sorting out any issues that they have. This approach helps when it's not possible to do what someone wants, and makes them happier when you can.

Becky Broome: Customer service is really important to us. We have processes in place to deal with situations that may arise but we add that personal touch wherever we can. A quick phone call to the customer to double-check their personalisation when a possible mistake has been spotted has been a great success. Not only are the customers delighted that you have taken the time to get in touch but it makes the whole process more personal. I always find that thinking like a customer and putting yourself in their position is the best way to deliver great customer service. Even if the customer isn't happy at first for one reason or another, customer service and how you deal with the situation is the biggest asset you have. Swift, efficient customer service can alter that customer's opinion and potentially gain you repeat orders.

Ellie Ellie: We always think about how we would respond to them if they were in our shop and this always sets a good visual for the structure of our customer service. We also think it is important for our customers to know we are also human – all our team have a signature sign-off that introduces them to the customers and lets them know their position in the company, plus two friendly facts about them. Some of our customer service team have become quite friendly with customers through this method. Lindsay (our Customer Service Team, Roller-Coaster Fanatic and Cat Lover!) was corresponding with a lady who had asked for Disneyland, Paris as her personalisation for one of her map cufflinks and on seeing that Lindsay was a roller-coaster fanatic suggested that if she fancied going to Disneyland to get back in touch to stay in her villa! Of course in addition to being human we do need a little help from technology, which enables us to keep customers informed by sending out emails once an order is confirmed and once it is dispatched. We strive always to keep the customer updated and informed. A strict process also keeps us on tip-top form, making sure every enquiry is answered within forty-eight hours, structurally formatting the order printouts to make sure we are getting out all our express orders quickly and always pushing to exceed customer expectation.

Delightful Living: A quick response to queries, listening and being receptive to a customer's point of view are important to us, as is showing appreciation of feedback whether good or bad. We find that a customer remembers how you deal with a complaint more than what the complaint was. If you take their views seriously and show you are human and want to help it usually diffuses any difficult situation.

What are you selling? You!

'I'm not a businessman, I'm a business, man!'

JAY Z

DAYS 23 TO 26

Growing your inspiration to sell; learning how to
make sure people are buying; the importance of feeling and
looking good; how to give presentations with confidence.

When we first started out, the initial successes and gains we made
came down to the way in which we sold ourselves as the owners and
creators of the business. Investors were as interested, if not more so,
in buying *us* as the brilliant idea we were bringing to them. The way
in which we presented ourselves to the potential partners mattered
more than the technical support and marketing savvy we were offering.
After all, it was always going to be down to us as to whether or not we
could run the business properly and bring them the returns on the
investment they needed or sell their goods. Bottom line: a great idea
run by incompetent people is going to fail; a so-so idea run by amazing
people will survive.

Once notonthehighstreet.com was up and running, much of our
growth depended on us and our story, whether it was to generate PR
or attract customers. Today we are hiring some of the best talent in
the world to come and work for us and we need to sell ourselves as
employers that will bring out the best in them and provide them with
the career opportunities they desire. In all these facets, the way in
which we talk about ourselves, present ourselves – *sell* ourselves, in
short – matters.

selling and
pitching

This chapter is less about the selling of an end product (that demands more in terms of connecting with customers, see The Customer, The Customer) and more about selling yourself. The brand you own or represent always comes down to you. You are the person to shape and nurture your brand – whether that's a personal brand, one you sell to people who employ you or whether it's a company you have founded or grown. You are also responsible for the people who will shape and nurture the brand alongside you. Think of brand leaders such as Karl Lagerfeld and Chanel, Richard Reed and Innocent, and Natalie Massenet and Net-A-Porter. Some people are invisible behind the brand yet still shape every tiny nuance of it: Mark Constantine, once of the Body Shop, went on to found Lush; Marcia Kilgore founded and grew Bliss spas then FitFlop. Once your brand and your relationship with it is nailed, you will easily identify and connect with your customer and you'll also be able to get to work refining your product so that you are selling them the thing they are motivated to buy from you.

Remember that when we talk about selling something, it's not necessarily a thing, a product – it could be a concept or idea, too. Anytime you are persuading another person to take something on, whether they pay for it or not, you are 'selling' to them.

Whatever you are selling, you must be emotive as well as rational. Whatever it is you want someone to buy, you will close the deal or make the sale only if you sell to the emotional part of the brain – and this applies to both men and women. (Men may incline towards the systematic approach but they still enjoy appeals to their emotions, whether something is sexy, makes them feel younger or makes them be a better dad; just as women may take the empathetic approach but are not averse to picking up a bargain.)

Of course, many of the lessons contained here can be applied to the direct selling of products. But when it comes to shaping yourself up and shaping up the business you're in, you need to pull yourself apart first. The bottom line is that when you ask customers or clients to buy into your business, it's *you* that closes the deal. You need to know if you are the right product for your customer. Do you have the right talents and experience? Are you getting yourself to market in the right way? Are you engaging usefully with social media, from Twitter to LinkedIn? Are you selling at the right price point or demanding the right fee? Is your brand right? What are your core values? Are these directing all your work? Have you got the right design? Is your personal image right for the business you're in?

We'll take you through these questions and help you find the answers that will reinvigorate your sales pitch, boosting your sales and your income.

But first off – and we make no apologies for this because we know how crucial it is to have a really positive personal presence – we're going to take a good look at you: your health, fitness and wardrobe. The fact is (and we know this can be a sensitive subject) that if *you* have not clearly bought into you, then it's a big ask of anyone else.

FIT FOR BUSINESS

Let's begin in the way we sometimes wish our weekends wouldn't: with a bracing workout. Call it 'a healthy start', if you prefer – and there's a first lesson in selling for you – but it's all about looking after yourself. Don't worry, this isn't about you having to squeeze into Lycra and sprinting round the park, this is just about being fit and well. There are two reasons this is an area of focus for us: first of all, it's so damn easy to neglect yourself at work; secondly, if you don't look fit, in tune with what's good for you and as though you're managing your own health, then people will look at you and wonder – what else is she missing?

When we first started the company, the long hours and intensity of what we were doing meant that concern for our physical wellbeing was forgotten. There wasn't a choice – we didn't choose to eat cake instead of going to the gym when we needed an energy boost, it was the only available option. At least, that's how it felt. It led to what our staff called 'the notonthehighstreet.com stone'. Google allegedly has the same problem and we don't doubt that anyone who has started up a business has watched their knicker elastic stretch over the weeks. Our huge fishbowls of sweets on every table didn't help matters – we soon got rid of them, pretty as they looked – but it was as much about the sheer need to be present in the office. The demand to work all hours meant we were rarely away from our desks at lunchtime – which equalled a lot of sitting on our bottoms eating sandwiches. Cakes at teatime when we knew we had far to go into the night. Revolting MSG-laden takeaways at midnight – yeuch, can still taste them now. Even if we escaped the office, we'd land at home, knackered, diving for the pizza and large glass of wine.

It took a while but eventually we took control. Now we find ourselves eating huge salads for lunch, exercising regularly and taking our downtime seriously. Neither we, nor the business, deserve anything less.

The current health mantra is 'fit not thin' and that's one we believe in. It's not about whether you're a size six or not – and we're certainly not – it's about how much energy you are getting from your own body. Exercise is work but exercise works. It clears your head, gets your blood pumping in a good way and speeds up your metabolism, thereby allowing you to enjoy that sneaky bar of chocolate without guilt. Best of all, it makes you feel good – proud of yourself that you are doing it at all and proud that you are hitting the targets you've set yourself (even if the profits have been falling of late). You'll walk into rooms with your back a little straighter, the energy shimmering around you. All that for thirty minutes a few times a week.

Sophie: 'When Holly and I first went on TV it was straight to national and the huge audiences of the BBC. It was, it goes without saying, fantastically exciting and a major coup for our PR programme. Professionally, it was a big achievement. But I wasn't happy with how I looked when I watched the playback afterwards. I saw someone who looked unfit, out of shape and tired. Ugh. I was being hard on myself. But it was how I felt, true or not, and it was a turning point. I realised that nothing was as important to the business, the family or myself as me feeling physically good. Unless I got fit, I could do no justice to those three pillars. It's taken four years of incredibly hard training and very early mornings to turn it around but it matters that I'm healthy and strong, a vital part of my confidence infrastructure. I train a lot now – five times a week, doing CrossFit, weight training and running – which I know isn't for everyone. But beginning the day feeling elated at the weight I've lifted, without a thought for the weight on the bathroom scales, means I perform better, make good, confident decisions and genuinely enjoy my working day.'

DAY 23, PART 1 PRACTICAL EXERCISE:
SCHEDULED FITNESS
allow: ten minutes

Commit yourself to an exercise programme and put it in your diary. It doesn't matter if it's a half-hour walk every other morning or a high-intensity indoor-cycle class once or twice a week.* Start small if you've not done much before – you don't want to set targets you can't achieve – but don't sell yourself short either. And make it a non-negotiable element of your schedule.

IMAGE

We hardly need to tell you – in our world of celebrity-obsessed magazines, ever increasing numbers of anti-ageing beauty products, Botox parties, purchase-and-return online clothes shopping and makeover TV shows – that looks matter. At least, that looks are judged.

We're not particularly interested in looking trendy, although we're always happy to reference a fashionable motif or pick up an accessory that makes our look current. It's about looking professional, stylish, smart and true to our brand. And in that we invest well, because our wardrobes are fundamental to our success, in how we feel and what we project. Whether you want to present yourself as a creative or as a board director, you need to think about what your clothes can say for you before you even start talking.

* For most of us, it's wise to think about checking with a doctor before starting any new exercise regime; in fact, we're obliged to tell you that.

And while we love the woman who can break all the rules and look like a complete original, that's not us – it's not most people, to be absolutely frank.

DAY 23, PART 2 PRACTICAL EXERCISE:
THE WARDROBE AUDIT
allow: three hours (then shopping!)

If you find it hard to do this alone, ask a friend to help you. First of all, you need to ruthlessly go through your wardrobe of clothes you'd wear for work and work-related events to clear it out, following these rules:

* If you never wear it, get rid of it.
* If it's ragged or old, get rid of it.
* If it fits badly or is uncomfortable, get rid of it. (If you plan to be in better shape soon, you will also deserve new clothes.)
* If it's dated, get rid of it. Be honest.
* If you wear it too much, like a pair of old slippers, and that shows, get rid of it.

Everything that's left probably includes things you love but don't wear enough. Line them up in your wardrobe and then wear them each in turn, a day at a time, in order, from today. Do not duck out or miss anything. If you repeatedly miss something out despite this rule, get rid of it. The only exception is when you know you'd wear it if you had the right thing to go with it.

If you are left with almost nothing in your wardrobe, then you had almost nothing anyway and you need to go shopping and shop well.

Next, shopping. Dressing yourself for business and making a statement doesn't need to break the bank – like running your business, you need to be practical, efficient and cost-savvy.

What you want to try to do is build your wardrobe in a way that reflects your personality appropriately for your business. Take time to think about what suits you, what feels comfortable and what makes you feel great. Think about what you want your clothes to say when you walk into a room because you will be as successful as you look and feel. There's another plus: investing thought and time says, 'I've been looking forward to seeing you, it's an occasion for me too.' That's flattering for whomever you are meeting and a good icebreaker.

Then, go shopping! Money spent here is an investment in the business so try to spend as much as you can afford.

We didn't start out as especially good shoppers, but with the help of some great advice from stylish friends, we've developed our own well-practised tricks of the trade that we stick to religiously:

✳ Know five or six shapes that suit you, whether trousers, skirt or dress, and look for those in different fabrics and colours.

✳ Get used to buying a really good investment piece now and then: Something about which there is absolutely no question that it was expensive, such as a really good jacket. It's not about being flash but conspicuously well made.

✳ Buy into your favourite pieces. If you've got a jacket, say, that you know you love but never wear, ask why you're not wearing it. Is it because you need trousers to go with it? Then buy them. Similarly, don't be put off from buying something stunning just because you have nothing to go with it. To the contrary, that's a great place to start an outfit.

✳ Having a 'uniform' approach is great and it keeps life simple. But make sure your staples are kept fresh and updated. Use accessories to turn a single outfit into different looks.

✳ Posh jumpers earn their keep far faster than evening wear, yet we tend to spend more on the latter. Prioritise good, everyday knitwear.

✳ It's fine to wear something on-trend and seasonal many times in a short period, then retire it.

✳ Buy more than you need – from shops with good returns policies – and take items back if they don't work. Knowing you will do this makes you bolder in the shop and stops the commitment phobia in its tracks.

✳ Don't even bother trying on the basics – buy in store but try them on at home with the relevant outfits. Again, check the returns policy first.

✳ Keep basics fresh – white shirts don't last and you need to keep refreshing them. You may not think they look tired but they will. Chuck anything that has a permanent stain anywhere.

✳ Invest in a good coat – you'll wear it almost every day (what else can you say that about?) and it's the definitive piece in making first impressions.

✳ The rule on impulse and sale buys: you can be adventurous if it's the type of garment you wear a lot. If you wear a blazer almost every day, you can indulge a frivolous, unexpected one so long as you truly love it. But don't fall in love with an unplanned dress if you never wear anything but trousers. It'll never come off its hanger in the wardrobe.

Every day is best; don't wait to wear it.

PRESENTING

The stakes are often extremely high when making a pitch or presenting. We know what it feels like for our entire future to rest on the next hour's meeting. Whether it's to get the job of a lifetime, secure financial backing or win a contract, it's always you that's up for sale. It's an on-the-frontline moment, with nowhere to hide. For many, it's the most terrifying aspect of work but there are ways to conquer the fear. We know.

We both have had a love/hate relationship with presentations over the years. We do see the value in a great presentation or speech and we've enjoyed watching many. Between us, we've also done a huge number of them ourselves, whether it was during our time in advertising or when we were pitching notonthehighstreet.com at the start, to potential investors and partners. As the company has grown and we have become increasingly recognised and rewarded for our work, we are asked almost daily to give talks, present awards or appear at an industry dinner or conference. In the beginning, being asked to give a talk was very flattering. This was quickly followed by the realisation that it was either too frightening to enjoy or, worse, a complete waste of everyone's time.

Still, the more we've done, the more confident we've become. That said, we both have very different approaches as to how we do them, which only goes to show what a clear reflection of one's personality and individuality presenting is.

One other point: the lessons in presenting should be applied to pitching on the phone or in a meeting – they really are all the same thing, just in a different environment. However, we are only talking about business-to-business pitches here – selling to consumers is an entirely different thing (see the chapter The Customer, The Customer for more on that).

Holly: 'I do a lot more public speaking now than I ever thought I would. Partly because I get asked to do some amazing, pinch-me events, and I just think it would be foolishness to turn them down. Talking for the Institute of Directors at the Royal Albert Hall before an audience of 3,000, for example. I never thought I could have done that but I have found my rhythm. I know now if I write a prepared speech it will be a disaster. So instead I have three cards with a couple of bullet points on each and I just go for it. I know that's how I do my best work and am accepted for me and that makes you more confident. Also, with experience has come the ability to say no to the things I know I can't talk about – I'm not your woman for a comment on a political situation. And it helps that I've seen very important, serious CEOs fluff their first three points. We're all human.'

Sophie: 'For every talk I do, I practise over and over again. I've been known to accept an invitation to make a speech for the sheer challenge of taking it on. I'll always aim to gain a boost to my confidence from the knowledge that I could do it. I know I need to have as many positive experiences as I can and I'll work to make them positive. But public speaking is one of my personal big hurdles. For me, that means working at it as hard as possible. Harder than at almost anything else because I am determined to get there.

'I've given speeches at some great events such as Innocent Inspires and Stylist Magazine Network that have gone really well, and that's made me feel good. I take the view that I want to give some fantastic talks over the course of my career so that I can be happy it didn't beat me. Maybe I'll stop the day that comes! In the meantime, I'll rehearse my way to confidence and a successful talk.'

PRACTICAL TIPS FOR SPEAKING SUCCESS

If you are asked to do a presentation – however informal or small the event – here are our top tips:

✳ Ask the organiser for details: what is the title and length of the talk? Do they expect any images or video? What is the technical set-up? Will you need to do a Q&A and will this be managed by the organisers or will you be fielding the questions alone? Do they require you to be present after the talk? How will you get there and how will you get home afterwards? What expenses will be covered? If you charge a fee, be upfront about this from the start.

✳ Whether you need every word rehearsed, like Sophie, or prefer just cues on a card, like Holly, at some point you need to think through the whole speech in its entirety. Sometimes it's helpful to write it out in full, then write the shorter version of it.

✳ Say it all out loud, even if it's just to yourself in the bath. It will give you a sense of the rhythm: when to stress a word, when to pause. If you need to rehearse meticulously, then do that to a trusted, experienced colleague, and really iron out the knots in some detail, so it flows and feels right. For Sophie, this is the difference between an okay talk and a good one.

✳ Don't worry about being funny. Some people naturally are and that's great, but most are not. Sometimes it's nice to have a break-the-ice line at the start, just to get the audience on your side but it's not why they're there to listen to you. Also, if you rely on laughter to gauge whether or not your audience is listening you'll lose heart very quickly as even professional comedians rarely get a laugh a minute, try as they might.

✳ Look as if you are enjoying yourself up there: smile, pause, step back from the lectern and look confidently at the room. If people feel you are okay standing up in front of them, they'll relax and listen. If you stare down at the lectern all the way through, no one will feel you're engaging with them and they'll stop listening.

DAY 24, PART 1 PRACTICAL EXERCISE:
BE RSVP-READY
allow: one hour

Draft an email that you can keep to hand, ready to top and tail to send to an organiser who asks you to deliver a speech. Include in it all the questions that you need to know the answers to before you can accept. Effectively, this email should contain your conditions for doing the presentation. You need to know whether it's something you want to do, if it's within your capabilities and if there is any value to you in doing it. Find this out by asking questions such as: who have the previous speakers at this event been? What media coverage will there be? How many will be attending? Who makes up the audience? Will there be opportunities to market or contact delegates afterwards? You can also include some questions from the tips above, such as subject, timing of talk and so on.

DAY 24, PART 2 PRACTICAL EXERCISE:
WATCH YOURSELF BACK
allow: three hours

Write a two-minute speech entitled: 'I feel confident when ...'. Practise writing it out in full, which means every single word you will say, from hello to thank you. Read it out loud to yourself. Then write down the shorter version on no more than one side of A4. Finally, write the speech on to no more than three cards with only bullet-pointed remarks.

Rehearse the speech to yourself then to someone else and ask for honest feedback about your delivery. Drawing on any past presentations too, make notes to yourself about what worked and what didn't: did you smile enough? Do you need a script or just cues? Do you prefer to walk about or do you need a lectern? And so on. Make sure you keep these notes somewhere you can refer to them quickly the next time you need to do a presentation. If you can bear it, get someone to video it. *Nothing* makes you correct your style more quickly and effectively than seeing every twitch, pause and um with your own eyes.

When it comes to presenting tools, such as PowerPoint or Keynote, it doesn't matter what you use, so long as you use something that enhances rather than distracts from your presentation. Use it well, do it with confidence and relevance and make sure that the main focus is you and what you're saying, not the display. Always rehearse the slideshow in advance and triple-check the A/V (audio-visual) set-up of wherever you are giving your talk in advance of the event itself.

THERE'S NO OFF SWITCH

The bottom line about being a person who owns their career or owns their business is that there is never a time when you are not selling, pitching or presenting in one form or another. If you're passionate about what you do, you'll always be *on*. That's when passion equals success. Tim Koegel is the author of *The Exceptional Presenter* and he rightly says that presentations are a part of everyone's life, every day and every minute. When you leave a message on voicemail, you're presenting yourself. When you're asking a mechanic for a price to fix your car, you're presenting yourself.

He also – and this is the bit we particularly like – makes the point that being an exceptional presenter isn't about being perfect, because we all make mistakes and that's natural and human. It's about making sure your message is understood. Koegel has a useful acronym to keep in mind, to help you guide your pitch or presentation: OPEN UP.

✳ Organised. **Make your message clear and compelling, easy to understand as well as sequential and logical.**

✳ Passionate. **Deliver your message with confidence – believe it, like it, look happy about it.**

✳ Engaging. **Connect with your audience often, using eye contact, names and moving around to keep their attention.**

✳ Natural. **Be conversational yet commanding. Avoid a speech that sounds scripted – if you know your material well, it will make it more personal.**

✳ Understand. **Know your audience (know your customer!). Connect early with the group that you need to persuade.**

✳ Practised. **Your skills need to be kept up even under pressure.** Koegel says: 'I've yet to find anybody who history considers to be an exceptional presenter who didn't *make* themselves exceptional. They worked at it and they made themselves exceptional. And you can practise your posture, relaxing your hand position, working on your eye contact, all day every day.

'Live the idea of making yourself a better presenter. Make it second nature. It's about you, learning to behave naturally but the right way.'

DAY 25 PRACTICAL EXERCISE:
ELIMINATE VERBAL GRAFFITI
allow: ongoing across a day, while carrying on as normal

Koegel calls 'verbal graffiti' the out-loud pauses that rain on any presentation – the 'you knows', 'ums', 'likes'. No one ever wrote these into any presidential speeches, did they? Try to go a minute, then an hour, then a day speaking without verbal graffiti. Do the same with your body language; practise good eye contact when talking to someone (anyone); watch your hand positions. Refresh and revisit every day. Remember you have to do something – or refrain from doing it – many, many times to make it a habit

BE MEMORABLE

When you're selling, whether it's you or your business, it helps to be memorable. But this can be hard to judge. A beautifully thought-out gift that references a past comment or meeting – that works. A memory stick with a logo on it – not so much. Of course you need to scale things to your budget and time frames but sometimes it's about little more than ensuring you've put your personal touch on something, whether it's a present, a thoughtful remark during a phone call or a pretty design element on a business plan. We always take gifts to important meetings, such as a personalised print from the site – but that's relevant because clever gifting is our business. The response is invariably a delighted, 'Oh, yes, bribery works!' Try to think of a few business icebreakers that you could do, things that reference the work you're in.

MEMORY

Remember those ads in the back of newspaper supplements, promising to improve your memory? We can't do the same here but we think it's worth focusing on memory for a moment as we believe it's a core part of business success.

Holly: 'Don't ask me to recite algorithms or key dates in history but I am able to pick up a conversation from previous days/weeks/years, whether a telephone call or a meeting, and recall it when I talk to that person again. I'm lucky but I also believe that being able to connect personally prior to selling is vital when it comes to establishing a bond, so I work on it too.'

Sophie: 'When I saw what a difference Holly's miraculous memory made to selling, and saw that she partly sought out those skills in the people she hired too, I learned from that. It became something I noticed and looked for in certain roles, a way of naturally distinguishing one type of employee from another and evaluating their potential. My own memory is different from Holly's – it's based on the deeply ingrained things. I'll recall something over and over again in order to get to the bottom of it and understand why it's important until it's distilled into something akin to a universal truth in my mind. That way, I'll never let it go. I also keep meticulous records and I know where to find them.'

These two approaches to memory are completely different but another reason the two of us complement each other well.

HOLLY'S MASTERCLASS ON SELLING AND PITCHING

Holly: 'As a born and bred saleswoman, I don't know if I have changed or become more accustomed to the fact that I'm always "on". Sales is passion – and vice versa. If you have a passion for something, you could say you are always "selling something", be it the new colour for the kitchen wall you want the person you live with to agree to or the dress that's double the cost you thought you were prepared to spend. Be it your business or the bank manager, you should always be in sales mode. It gets you places faster and people appreciate passion.'

* **Be credible.** If you're selling to someone, they want to know why you are worthy of their investment (whether time, money or employment). Ensure you have worked out the answer to this, first and foremost.
* **Stick to the truth.** No fudging, no hiding. If there's an elephant in the room, someone will ask you about it – be prepared to give the right and honest answer.
* **Be slick not sloppy.** Figures should be consistent, slides triple-checked, names correct.
* **Take knocks – but keep coming back.** Tenacity gets you everywhere.
* **Adapt to survive.** Become the person you are selling to – whether it's the VC, customer or bank manager, put yourself in their shoes. Answer the questions you know they have on their mind.
* **Don't be shy.** Be persuasive and knowledgeable.
* **Don't understand the word 'no'.** This drives Holly's partner mad but any so-called obstruction is, for her, just a problem to be solved.

* **Don't dwell.** Move forward. This skill will help you quickly overcome anything thrown at you, however unexpected.
* **Know it.** Whether pitching your business in order to hire the right person or selling a product – it equals sales.
* **Be yourself.** Always. But know who you are first.

RELATIONS WITH YOUR PUBLIC

Whether it's the company you work for or the company you own, at some point you will need to engage in PR (public relations). We have found it a vital part of the sales process and at the centre of it, more than any other communication channel, is you. Articles in magazines and newspapers, whether regional, national or online, are a showcase for your achievements as well as a great way to reach your target demographic without paying for advertising. A portfolio of press cuttings is also a quick way to demonstrate to any potential investor that your company has appeal.

If you're a small company with a limited budget, you may be doing your own PR and that's fine. If you're feeling a bit stuck, try to get some expert advice in, if not for free then for a day's rate of pay.

News and feature journalists are always looking for a story and that is what you need to give them. When we started out, we conducted and published our own small-business market research so that we had something to talk about. We presented the results to the media, government and captains of industry and by the end of the first year we had appeared in almost every national newspaper, supplement and women's glossy magazine.

You can also target more niche journalists, particularly online with its wealth of bloggers and reviewers. Find the ones who write about your kind of business and target them. The audiences might be smaller than those of, say, a national newspaper, but they'll be exactly right for you. Focusing on four or five publications that are likely to run your story is far better than blanketing every single one with a press release.

Be prepared – know the details of your product or service, from price to availability. Have photographs that can be emailed or uploaded to the picture desk as soon as they are requested. Make sure they are the right format and size, as well as correctly captioned. Remember to think about seasonality – a monthly magazine is prepared three to four months before it comes out. You can always embargo a press release – that is, set a timing deadline as to when that information may be published.

From a personal image point of view, keep in mind that any interview with a journalist will take in the whole picture. Think about what image it is that you want to present to the readers of the publication or viewers of the television show.

For any interview, pre-plan the three key messages you want to put across. Stick to your story – there's no need to tell them about things they don't ask about, whether it's your childhood or your views on the royal family, unless they are absolutely relevant. Remember that you can deflect questions if you're not happy answering them and everything you say – from hello to goodbye – is on the record.

Sophie: 'We've come a long way since that first TV appearance. We've since done media training and hundreds of interviews, and we know the importance of being prepared. Interview requests can come at a moment's notice – sometimes literally. We were invited by the Cabinet Office last year to form part of a small panel of entrepreneurs speaking to the press. We'd prepared statements, were well dressed, calm and ready … but what we weren't expecting was that immediately afterwards we were asked to do six solo pieces to camera, one after another, to a multitude of TV and news channels, as well as radio interviews and a photo call. It was a whirlwind that might have thrown us in the early days, but we walked away with a big sigh of relief that we'd successfully pulled it off. That was a day that we felt we'd truly cracked it.'

DAY 26 PRACTICAL EXERCISE:
BE INTERVIEW-READY
allow: three hours

We've learned that there's much you can do to be always at the ready when you get that call you've worked so hard for, and if you are it pays off in spades.

Get an outfit lined up

Do this now. You can be sure that when the time comes, you won't have time to go shopping. It should, of course, say all the right things about you and your business. We can't tell you what that should be but make sure it is:

* Representative of what you do. Commercial, creative or otherwise.
* Comfortable and fits well. You do not want to be pulling and straightening things in the middle of or just before an interview.
* Smart, clean, pressed, new-looking, as well as complete with accessories and unladdered tights.
* Simple and, if for TV, not bright white, nor with a big or geometric pattern and not stripy. Tailoring – jacket or dress – are a safe bet, especially for camera.

From now on, by all means wear this outfit from time to time – don't waste it! – but be sure that it's the one set of clothes that you always have in your wardrobe and ready to wear (not stuck at the dry-cleaners).

Prepare a media pack
You'll need this both before and when attending an interview with a journalist and, like the outfit, you're unlikely to have time to put it together at the moment that it's needed.

* It should contain an up-to-date, general background press release, stating what your company does, key personnel, your role and any vital facts, like number of employees, awards won, major events, date the company was established. It should also include an up-to-date, good-quality photo of you and, if relevant, one or two photos of your key products or a current brochure or catalogue. Plus the usual contact details at the end of the release.

✳ Print out two or three good-quality copies – not too many as it will date – and put in a supply of folders, as well as creating a digital copy, with the files correctly labelled. The photo should be titled with the caption you would want to be used: your name, job title, company name.

✳ Learn all the information by heart. You should be able to deliver it off the cuff.

✳ Email the pack to the journalist in advance of any interview, so they know about you when they meet you. Also take a hard copy with you, because they may not have looked at it yet (don't be offended!), plus it's always good to leave a takeaway.

Stage a mock interview. Get a friend to help

Even if you're not going on camera, it's a good idea to work on the basis that your interview is live and being filmed, because the principles of readiness and coming across well in an interview apply in every situation, including sitting in a room with the journalist or even talking on the phone.

✳ Decide on the subject of your mock interview. Your latest product collection or new project launch is good.

✳ Put together a postcard with some background key stats about your industry such as the overall annual value and growth rate. Two or three stats at most. Any more and you will feel overwhelmed and forget them. These are simply for context, so you can show why your sector is important and how your business stands out within its industry.

✳ Prepare two key points that you want to make about your business. What do *you* want to say (regardless of what you're asked)? For example, that your company is the leading distributor of locally grown organic fruit in the UK. And that you're the only brand to show the food miles for every product.

✳ For those two points, prepare two examples or illustrations that show that they are true. If you possibly can, make these personal or very real. Bring them to life by talking about the present and about real people. For example: 'Only yesterday we provided 30,000 UK households with locally farmed organic apples'; 'I had an email from a customer this morning who told me she likes our brand best because we actually show the number of miles the food has travelled on every pack.'

✳ Set up your movie camera (a phone is fine) and get your friend to start asking you questions and filming you. They should ask you to introduce yourself and your company, and ask a very general question about your industry or business.

✳ The important part is to practise turning those questions into saying the things *you* want to say.

✳ Watch the movie. It will tell you clear as day what you need to do and what you need to improve. Don't shy away from it. Spend time ironing out your glitches and practise, practise, practise.

AWARDS

Awards are a part of PR too. They are also, of course, moments – when your work or your company's achievements have been recognised by either your peer group or customers – but equally they are useful things to publicise more widely. Quite simply, they let everyone else know that what you do has been validated and approved. For your business, awards are a great motivator before you've even won – they help set the benchmark so that you and your team understand where you need to get to.

Over the years, we are giddily proud to say, we have been nominated for – and won – many awards, from Essence of the Entrepreneur to Women of The Future. But as much as we enjoyed those trophies (and celebration parties!) we have to admit that nothing came close to the moment we discovered we had each been awarded an MBE for our services to small businesses and entrepreneurs in the UK.

Sophie: 'My letter came first. Underwhelmingly, it looks like a tax statement. "On Her Majesty's Service" stamped on the brown envelope. I opened it and immediately welled up, ran upstairs to show Simon, who also welled up. You are sworn to secrecy and, while it seemed logical that Holly would get a letter too, I didn't want to spoil the moment for her, so I just texted her to say, "Is Frank at home to check the post right now?" Of course, she guessed something big was up. Her letter then didn't come for three days, on all of which either Holly or Frank was hanging off the doorstep waiting for the postman. Finally, the letter came and Holly tore it open and kissed the postman. I'm guessing she eventually told him why!

'That's the best bit, getting the letter and having to keep it secret until it's announced in the Birthday Honours List in the press a few weeks later. When it was published, we were able to finally tell the staff, our partners, the board, our extended families and our friends and thank them all because we truly and genuinely – not like over-dramatic Oscar winners – know that our MBEs are a tribute to them and their hard work, loyalty and talent.'

After the notification of the MBE itself comes the invitation. Our ceremony was to take place at Windsor Castle, rather than Buckingham Palace, which turned out unexpectedly to be one of the best things about it. The number one concern was, clearly, our outfits; we swear, it's like getting married. Holly wore a beautiful navy Goat dress and Sophie wore a navy and lime creation by Preen. Choosing those only took, oh, about fifteen shopping trips each. We tried to read all we could about the event so that we were prepared – from protocol to timings – but it's surprisingly hard to find that last tiny detail about how to conduct yourself on this very specific occasion.

We were both unbelievably nervous, especially once we were chatting to the staff at Windsor and one of them told us that it was 'the boss' conducting the investiture. We were separated from our guests – limited to no more than three each, which was probably a lifesaver or our entire extended families would have been getting in on it – and sent up the stairs to the briefing room. We were thrilled to see we were in the company of comedian Rob Brydon and designer Emma Bridgewater (who was there under another name). All the staff were charming and lovely, making us feel very special, always saying things such as 'It's your day, of course you can!' when we did things like ask for water after it had all been put away!

As you would expect with a British royal occasion, every single thing was immaculately organised and we were all very well looked after. We were taken through the drill – a fairly simple combination of walks, stops and words. Then it was just us ... and HM The Queen.

Sophie: 'I practised and practised, became increasingly convinced that I was going to fall over when I curtseyed but when it was finally time, I managed to do as I was told – walk this way, stand next to this person, do what he says, walk forward, stop, turn, curtsey, walk forward, stop in front of the Queen (this was where I stopped breathing), address her as "Your Majesty" the first time, then "Ma'am" from then on. The Queen herself looked immaculate and radiant, was charming, chatted to us both and even made the connection between Holly and me although we were about twenty places apart in the line. When she has pinned on your medal and shaken your hand, you're supposed to walk backwards, curtsey again, then turn and leave the room.

'I thought I did okay. At first. As okay as you can feel when you've stopped breathing for quite some time. And haven't eaten for at least eighteen hours. And believe that your stiletto is destined with complete and utter certainty to get stuck in the carpet and bring you over in a display of airborne gymnastics. Which, needless to say, it didn't. Then, when I was a few feet out of the room I realised with a bolt that I hadn't done the second curtsey. Or maybe I had. I hoped I had. I was ushered to a row of seats to see the last few moments of the ceremony before it ended and a very smart, handsomely dressed member of the royal household looked over at me, smiled, and said, "I believe you have an appointment in the Tower." I was in such a spin, I think I believed him.

'Afterwards we had interviews with the press, then I went back to our favourite local restaurant, for lunch with my extended family. When I got home my ten closest friends were waiting for me. It was a milestone day – like marriage and the birth of my children – I'll never forget it or stop being grateful for it'

Holly: 'The day of our MBE was so special, like a wedding but without all the headaches – well, apart from the outfit trauma! For me, it started with a very early wake-up call and a hairdresser trying to tame my hair. My dear Frank and family took it upon themselves to really spoil me. Ironically, I was going through a tough time at work with Christmas at its peak, issues that needed solving – the very long year had caught up on me and I found myself worrying a great deal the day before. Every time I thought about what was about to happen I'd cry even more – then more again because my eyes were going to be like slits!

'Finally, on the morning, when I was ready, Frank opened the door to reveal the Bentley and chauffeur he had hired for the day! I remember telling – ordering! – myself to soak up every single moment I'll always remember laughing with Sophie when we were waiting. The moment came when I was next in line and I spied Frank, my sister Carrie and my son Harry. I teared up again but thankfully this time was able to hold it together. I mentioned to the Queen that I had showed her around my school when I was head girl aged seventeen and what an honour it was to meet her again. I walked away beaming and with my head held high. I think that this is the only time in my life other than giving birth to Harry that I've been truly proud of myself. We drove away listening to Kiss FM and singing loudly. When we got home, I was surprised again with red, white and blue balloons, a table spread with a Union Jack cloth and three boxes with MBE beautifully written on the front. We ate fish and chips in Union Jack paper bags and drank fizz. Little did I know that even this was only the start of my family making me feel so special. Carrie had arranged all my nearest and dearest to write a note of what I meant to them, from my first boss to partners, old friends and my son! I cried lots and lots more! And if all that wasn't enough, Frank whisked me off to Paris for the weekend. All in all the second most memorable day of my life.'

WE ASKED OUR PARTNERS

Do you like doing pitches, interviews, talks and presentations? What's your top tip?

Bookishly: I do enjoy presenting and my top tip is to be *really* prepared. It sounds obvious but if you have researched everything and practised, it will give you a huge amount of confidence. I am proud of my business and I know it inside out so talking about it is never a problem!

Pearl and Earl: My top tip is empathy and passion. Know what it is that they want or need to hear so it is appropriate. How passionate you are about the subject or your business will always be infectious.

Sophia Victoria Joy: Although it's not the norm for me to do pitches and presentations I do feel confident and enjoy speaking. I feel that being open and honest with a subject such as my own business gives the confidence required to give a great pitch. Prepare thoroughly and know the subject inside out. You know better than anyone in the room the ins and outs of your business and they are there to listen and learn from you, so you should have every confidence in your ability.

Delightful Living: I enjoy face-to-face pitches and interviews but do shy away from talks and presentations due to nerves! My tip would be to prepare as much as possible. You should feel confident in the knowledge that you know your product better than anyone else, but make sure you have all your facts and figures to back you up in answering questions. If you believe in your business and your products then your genuine enthusiasm for both should shine through.

Do you consciously dress in a way that reflects your business?
Have you changed the way you dress as your business has grown?

Bookishly: I wear my own jewellery all the time now! In the creative industries we are not expected to be in business suits all the time, so it is not difficult to be comfortable.

Ellie Ellie: The branding of Ellie Ellie is a direct reflection of a passion to be sustainable, creative and personal. My clothing therefore reflects my business, as well as my business reflecting me.

Pearl and Earl: I haven't adapted my style to the business. As I have grown older I am less 'fashion' and more my own personal style. Which is brand reflective anyway. Being yourself is key.

Sophia Victoria Joy: I am interested in trends and enjoy updating my wardrobe with fresh new colours and styles. I don't feel any pressure to dress a certain way to impress my peers. I always feel comfortable in what I am wearing and I want those looking at me to feel that my business and I are accessible.

Delightful Living: The Delightful Living overall brand and products are very much a reflection of our own tastes, home and lifestyle and how we dress is a part of that. We sometimes find ourselves subconsciously dressing in the same colours as a new product range or designing products in the same colour as a new outfit. I don't think we have changed the way we dress as the business has grown, but appearance is important to both of us and we like to give a 'delightful' first impression.

Making it work at home

'For most of history, Anonymous was a woman.'

VIRGINIA WOOLF

DAYS 27 TO 28

In which we get personal about how we struggle with –
and occasionally win – the battle between our
domestic and professional demands.

Remember the famous adage 'Behind every great man, there stands a great woman'? But what if it's a great woman out front – does she have a great man behind her? This is the twenty-first-century crisis (or conundrum, depending on your point of view). There is, in the developed world at least, agreement that men and women are equal and should be given equal access to education, political leadership, career opportunities and pay. But it is still also true that women do 80 per cent more housework than men and there are only four female CEOs in FTSE 100 companies. We haven't got there yet.

In the meantime, our generation is fighting the battle for culture change. One that will lead, we hope, to couples – whether gay or straight – sharing an equal division of labour in the home, enabling each other to go to work fully supported and feeling the opposite of bedraggled (which is, generally, how we feel first thing on a Wednesday morning, halfway through the long working week).

Since our first book *Build a Business from Your Kitchen Table* came out, Simon, like Frank, has become a househusband so now both have given up their jobs to support us (and our children) at home. Has it worked? We'll come back to that.

finding
balance

Sometimes it feels as if we're fighting DNA. We've lost our right to micromanage the house, the children, even Christmas. We're getting used to it now, but when we come home at night, it can still feel downright weird to hear our husbands moan about the difficulties of keeping on top of the laundry, complaining that the dog needs to go the vet, the dishwasher is leaking and what with the children's sports day to prepare for they just haven't got the *time*. We have to remember how stressful all that is and avoid eye-rolling in response, knowing our week is back to back with meetings, finance planning, PR events and a thousand countless questions that will need to be answered responsibly to our various employees and partners, each one of whom is expecting us to muster full-strength enthusiasm and foolproof knowledge in our responses and actions. Basically, it's a 1950s sitcom, in reverse.

But we feel strongly that it's something we need to talk about and work out. Because unless women feel that they have the freedom of choice to go out and work, unless men feel that they have the freedom of choice to stay at home and raise the children, unless both partners feel that they are able to share fairly the domestic tasks ... nothing will change. Running a business or scaling the heights of your ambition while simultaneously trying to order an online supermarket shop, pack lunches, hoover the hallway and shave your legs ahead of date night is simply not possible. Or, it is possible but will lead to burnout at worst, a breakdown on holiday at best.

We also need to talk about the fact that it's about far more than simply being given choice. Equality of choice is not enough to redress the balance. Technically, we've already achieved equality in terms of legislation. Today, the problems come increasingly down to a deep

cultural issue: it takes courage to speak out and acknowledge that
working is different for parents, yes, but – this is the daring part,
perhaps a little out of bounds in terms of political correctness – to
say that it is especially so for female parents. Because only when
we acknowledge that difference can we do something about it, and
expect industry and society to do something about it too. For instance,
Cancer Research UK has started to recognise that it is losing some of
its strongest, most talented scientists – ones who are getting us to a
cure, sooner – because the demands of a major breakthrough study can
make life impossible for the scientist (and coincidentally mother) who
is leading it. So having recognised it, CRUK is doing something about it
with their Women of Influence campaign. Equality is only half the story
and we're happy to say that the next, vital part of the conversation is
underway. Equal *and* different is what's now on the agenda.

That said, we're not just talking about motherhood here. Relationships
need nurturing and care if they are to survive. Both partners need to
feel supported and respected in their ventures if they are to do them
well. Nor are we even talking about just those in marriage or civil
partnerships; single women need support too. If you are single, do
you have the friends that can see you through the bad times as well as
celebrate the good? Do you have the support from wider family and
friends that enables you to prioritise your work when you need to?
Women are often the ones who get given the responsibility of looking
after ageing parents; single women are expected to step in frequently
to help with nieces and nephews or even godchildren. Women are said
to be better nurturers of relationships, to be more adept at looking
after extended family, and often it feels that we are – certainly, we
enjoy it. We want to be there for those who need us and it pains us,

hugely, when we can't be. But when can we give ourselves permission to prioritise our work? And when do we need to prioritise ourselves, our family, our friends? Our health, sanity and wellbeing will affect our business. We'll examine this holistic approach or at least, its ideal – we know we rarely attain it.

So. Making it work at home. We're not going to tell you how to organise your personal life – you might live alone, with your children, sometimes with children and sometimes without, sometimes with a partner and sometimes without, with a dog, with chickens, with ferrets. Anything goes. And that's great. But while we don't care what you get up to behind your own front door, we do care that women are not always good at asking for help, and we don't believe that you can make it in business unless you have a very strong support network.

Everyone needs their own personal army with foot soldiers ready to come marching quickstep to your aid when you need them. That might be the friend who always bolsters your confidence, the colleague who is a brilliant problem solver, the husband who cooks all your suppers so you don't have to, the fabulous childminder who takes care of the children, the nursery that is flexible about last-minute hours or the dog-walker always at the ready. You could include in this retinue a personal stylist, a hairdresser who always gets it exactly right or a personal trainer who leaves you feeling invigorated and strong. We hope, too, that you provide one of these bolstering services to someone else, even if it's just listening when the SOS call is sent out.

DAY 27 PRACTICAL EXERCISE:
AUDIT YOUR SUPPORT NETWORK
allow: one hour

Take an hour to think about to whom you can turn when you need help, both personal and professional. From the childminder to the friend who will collect the children from school if you are stuck; the IT man who you can call when your computer crashes or the service that delivers fast replacement ink for your printer. Which hairdresser gives you the best results when you need to feel good and have you got a decent seamstress to fix a loose hem or tear in your favourite dress? What friend can understand and explain tax returns and which will pour a large glass of wine and listen sympathetically? Gather all their names, email addresses and telephone numbers on to a single list and have it saved on your desktop, with maybe a copy handy in case anyone else needs it. That's your support network - you may not call on it too often but it will always help to know it's there.

We've both been very lucky in that throughout the start-up and growth of notonthehighstreet.com we've been with partners, raising our children and running our homes together. We have a great support network of friends, nannies at times, and our families are, for the most part, either close by or actually working with us in the office. While we're both fiercely independent and ambitious and want our own success on our own terms, we've never been afraid to reach out for help when we've needed it, or to say that it's something that's well worth paying for, perhaps even over other things that some might consider more worthy.

It's also been a significant factor in our success that we have always had each other to turn to when it comes to the business – we've never kept secrets and we've pledged to be candid when it comes to letting the other know how we feel about any turn of events. Sometimes that is easier said than done: you have to be strong to show weakness. But it's always paid off, even if it's just a hug of reassurance that things will turn out okay.

Still, there have been low moments when the struggle to stay on top at work and be the mother/wife/daughter/sister/friend that we want to be threatens to pull us apart into tiny, shattered pieces. It's taken that mess to tell us that we have to make serious changes and while we can't tell you what you need to do to make changes, we do want you to watch out for the warning signs and tackle it before it turns into an emergency.

We know that you will feel that you must be brilliant at everything because when you're setting yourself incredibly high standards at work it's hard to change your behaviour at home. But no one can be amazing at every single thing, all the time. Most of us know that. The dilemma is how to resolve this – whether you do everything yourself, share it or farm it out, each solution is flawed. We do think that tackling things jointly with your partner if you have a family to look after has one very important outcome, even if you get things wrong: you will be teaching future generations the importance of sharing responsibility and doing things together. We don't claim to have got it right yet either personally or as a nation – childcare being still both ridiculously underfunded and overpriced – but in trying we hope our sons and daughters will grow up expecting to raise their families with their wives or husbands as teams, not as sole agents with completely different responsibilities.

As all home lives are unique, we'll tell ours individually.

Sophie: 'My children, Honor and Ollie, were young when we started the business – six and eight years old, respectively – and when we had no money to spare, childcare was a patchy nightmare, largely consisting of miserable breakfast clubs before school and either Simon or I racing home to be with them for supper and homework. Then we got a fabulous nanny and she stayed with us for years, making everything okay again and even training our puppy, Rufus, into a well-behaved dog complete with a repertoire of tricks. After she left, the children were eleven and thirteen years old and the difficult thing about that kind of age is that there's no real childcare solution. For the most part, the evenings were dealt with because both had a lot of homework to do and then Simon would get home in time to check in with them and feed them. If he had clients to meet and I was trapped in the office, we were lucky enough to have various friends who could help out: from our next-door neighbour, who would take them, feed them, nag them about homework and generally make them feel part of the family; to my mum taking them away to Wales for a week every summer. Simon usually did the evenings and I did the mornings, and in that way we got by for two more years.

'Or, we thought we did. In the summer of 2012, our children were fifteen and thirteen, reaching a whole new level of independence and Simon and I anticipated things getting much easier. Yet, we suddenly, collectively, were absolutely broken at the end of what we, perhaps smugly, had considered a frankly extraordinary run of both parents working intense hours in relentlessly demanding jobs while – more or less – keeping family life together.

'So I had kind of thought we were okay. Now and then, I'd catch a sick feeling at the bottom of my stomach, knowing they were really quite neglected at times. More times than I can bear to think of now, I'd get a slightly bleak text from Honor at eight or even nine o'clock, asking, "Is there any food for us?" I'd frantically try to get in touch with Simon to begin an exchange of "I thought you were home tonight?" or "I told you it was going to be a late night … where are you?" that would usually end in one of us trying to get a meal/homework support/lift somewhere organised by remote control. None of which exactly made us soar with pride about our parenting.

'The turning point was a conversation I had with a friend, someone I greatly admire, who works for a local charity. As she described the work of the charity, I felt that sick feeling in my stomach. The purpose of this charity was directed at families, supporting those in unhappy domestic circumstances, where children were neglected or under extreme stress. But not the locked-in-the-shed-and-starved types that one imagines. No, she was talking about the surprisingly high prevalence of clinically depressed, starved-of-attention middle-class children in our area. Where parents worked long, long hours and children – young adults but not really adults at all – were left to fend for themselves while under high pressure at school. As I listened, feeling tearful, a rush of horribly familiar feelings that I had pushed to the back of my mind rose up. I suddenly knew our current situation couldn't continue. There were *charities* to protect children like mine?

'In hindsight, I was overreacting, it wasn't that bad. But it was bad enough for me – I didn't want my children suffering even half as much as those children were. So Simon and I discussed it and discovered that he was open to the idea of leaving work to run the house and look after the children. He'd had thirty successful years in the City but it had been getting tougher all the time since the recession bit. He was ready for a sabbatical and given that his domestic skills are far better than mine, it was logical.

'Which is not to say it's instantly been a bed of roses. While the children will tell us that they found it miserable at times, being latchkey kids, they also clearly enjoyed the independence and privileges that our absence brought them, whether it was an uninterrupted hour or two of watching trashy TV or delaying homework to the last possible moment. Nor have I been allowed – now that one of us is there to police them – to simply remove these privileges from Honor and Ollie, thanks to their spirited defence. Good for them, I reckon.

'But Simon and I found it unexpectedly difficult to adjust too. For the most part, I worried that Simon wasn't happy or would suddenly feel unfulfilled or depressed (I know I would) but luckily he's pretty easy-going on that front. We squabbled a bit about how things should be done but any woman letting go of her domestic remit is going to struggle. That said, it's those areas that are easier to define and parcel up. Simon cooks – and shops – and I don't interfere in that at all because he's so much better at it than I am. He also looks after the animals, the recycling and so many other things now that are in his remit. I am superior when it comes to laundry and more inclined to keep tabs on the children when there's a lot of homework to do.

'Then, after a year of Simon at home and me in the office, it's changed again. I'm based at home more and we've had to work over things once again, marking out our territories and respecting each other's priorities.

Above all else, though, we both feel very fortunate to be in this position at all. Simon relishes his role – he always was the best at organising things socially, as well as holidays, simply getting us all out there to enjoy what life has to offer. We can also enjoy each other a bit more – at last – and no more sleep is lost worrying that our children are neglected.'

Holly: 'Frank left his twenty-two-year career with the Metropolitan Police in 2011 after a disastrous nanny – so terrible she only lasted seven days – and we both decided we needed consistent childcare but couldn't risk another mistake. With the business taking off, it made sense for Frank to be the one to stay at home with Harry, by now five years old. But it was much, much harder than either of us anticipated.

'After being an independent working man, Frank found it very difficult to adjust to days of looking after a small boy – doing the school run, never-ending wash loads, dry-cleaning to pick up and homework to get done. We had sort of expected that, though, and muddled through it. The biggest shock was for me – I suddenly realised that I had lost the right-hand women I'd always had in my nannies for five years. It took away my ability to run the house, to decide if Harry was well enough to go to school, to make sure there were enough vegetables on his plate and how the house looked.

'This put huge pressure on our relationship, I think because our roles had swapped so completely. It felt at times as if we were trying to push back against our natural instincts, and losing. What I've now realised, three years in and into my fourth, is that if I am unable to contribute to my family in the week, it affects me at work. So I have to have that balance, I have to find it somewhere. Frank has to let me ask him about Harry's breakfast or the vegetables, or let me decide whether he should or shouldn't go to rugby. I cannot give up my right to be the nurturer just because I'm a woman who goes to work. It short-circuits me and I explode – or, worse, I implode and turn it all on myself.

'We know now that you cannot "have it all". If you try, something will give and that's usually yourself. Far better to try and find practical measures that can be put in place to stop that happening.

'For me, the solution – or a part of reaching for the solution – is realising that those traditional roles do work and you have to try to make them fit into modern life. A man needs to provide, so if he's the one at home, there must be some other way of him being that provider. Women need to nurture, so even those at work all week must be allowed to do that when they get home at the weekend.

'That's on my radar now, which is not to say it's solved things. But I do recognise the danger signs – bickering is one of them, particularly if we're sweating over the small stuff. Also, Harry is – like all children – a great barometer. If he's having arguments at school, that means he's not happy and I need to spend more quality time with him. It's okay to say that he needs "Mummy love", even if Mummy is not the main carer.

'Things are more settled as we go into our fourth year of this set-up but I'd say the dust is still settling and it's only now I realise that it takes this long. The most important thing is that you take extra care of the relationship. The woman normally does this and if roles have changed, then you risk not having that time to make things "right". It's all very well to expect the man to do this but I think you have to cut them a break. They are battling – whether they admit it or not – with their DNA,

246

caveman, provider issues, call it what you will, and there is no point in landing them with the nurturer/fixer/Mummy role too!

'If you work and the roles have changed, accept that you need to be the ultimate carer of the relationship. Step in, check in, make sure men feel like men, get help in the house where needed if you can. Accept that it needs you to make things better and help evolution along! Frank now volunteers for Age Concern, is key to our family project of building a school in Africa and is considering a couple of consultancy roles, which would allow him to work around our family.'

DAY 28 PRACTICAL EXERCISE:
DO NOTHING!
allow: a whole day ...

Yes, that's right. Have one day to tell yourself you're coping just fine and *not* trying to do everything and be perfect. Reflect on the good things, whether that's your children, your home, your newly painted nails or the supper you've got planned. It's been proven again and again that happiness is increased when people make a regular note of what good things happened to them that day or week. So remember to take time out now and then to do this. It's easy to focus on the negative events or critical comments and sometimes you must, of course, address things that need to be fixed, as we've discussed at length in this book. But you must also remember what works, what you enjoy, what makes you tick – and keep on doing it.

WE ASKED OUR PARTNERS

How do you cope with the tug-of-war between work and home?

Highland Angel: When my work/life balance is on the scales, the work side is definitely too heavy! Highland Angel has grown rapidly, so we no sooner have enough staff than we get busier and need more. I'm lucky that my children are grown up and work with me, along with my husband so when we're busy we all help out This means I don't have to feel guilty about putting work before my family.

Delightful Living: Our premises are just how we imagined they would be. In the early days while working from the kitchen table and garden shed, we dreamed of a 'delightful' converted dairy, space to bring our two dogs to work and a rural outlook. We now work from The Old Cow Shed, a converted cow shed and milking parlour on a farm in rural Derbyshire with our two dogs by our side.

A Piece Of: We always wanted our business to do well, of course, but when we started it, we thought we could manage to work on a part-time basis around children and other jobs. Quickly we realised that this wasn't the case; if we wanted the business to go forward we had to put the hours in.

Sophia Victoria Joy: On the whole the great freedom that I wanted in running my own business is just as I had imagined it and it's really rewarding. I judge how much I love what I am doing by how I feel about it on a Sunday night; do I get the dreaded feeling of knowing it's Monday morning tomorrow or not? So far I haven't had this once while I have been running my business, which I see as a good sign!

Pearl and Earl: The only pain is working with your spouse! He will say the same back. They don't listen and you have to leave your marriage at home. I would *never* recommend it – but we have made it successfully work over the years. Being a woman at work doesn't make a difference but being a mum does. I started the business pregnant with my first child and then had my second. There was no maternity leave for me. (My advice is have your babies when you still have your day job and maternity leave.) In that respect it is hard juggling everything and dealing with the guilt.

How did you do?

'Sometimes success demands a certain refined insanity.'

ISOBELLE CARMODY

DAYS 29 TO 30

Falling in love with your business all over again.

In the early days, when you are first dreaming about your business, success seems easy to define. You imagine total contentment washing over you like the tide on a warm beach the first time you turn over half a million pounds/move into an office/get your first article in the paper/run a TV ad/ your father calls and tells you how impressed he is/pay for a two-week, five-star holiday to the Caribbean ...

Whether one of these things happens, or some of them or even all of them there's only one guarantee – you won't recognise the moment of 'success'. It certainly won't feel like you thought it would. This is not to say that you won't enjoy those moments when they arrive – you will. But there will be an underlying tinge to them – the worry about the things that aren't quite right yet, the knowledge that now there's further to go because the goalposts keep moving, the added pressures of running something that is bigger, messier and more complicated than you knew it would be.

We have enjoyed our success. We love the awards, the contentment that comes with having created a business that others benefit from – whether employee, partner or customer – and the financial rewards have made life easier for our families. All that is good. But certain things don't change. Your imposter syndrome gets bigger. Or you find

your progress

yourself concentrating on trying to fulfil a vision of yourself so as not to slip back to the other, more familiar, negative vision. Fear remains a driver.

But how can you combat this? Is there a point at which you are able to say 'I've got – or done – enough, I no longer need to be afraid'?

If you are feeling overwhelmed by the responsibilities and pressures, then take a walk on the wild side: ask yourself what would happen if you left your business? Just a quick mental snapshot should be enough to remind yourself that you and your business not only need each other but do each other good too.

Something else also happens when your business is successful: you're no longer creating but maintaining. The creative vision that kept you going is replaced by the daily grind. That can lead to many business owners falling out of love with the very thing they gave birth to. You need tactics that will keep you going and help you fall in love with your business again. Staying fresh is vital.

We find that we can draw great strength from reflecting on recent successes and great moments. It's important to create situations where you *have* to do that. So we have our annual review speech, which we make to everyone who works at notonthehighstreet.com. Usually, when it comes around, we find we're writing the speech in a rush, simultaneously dealing with a ton of other urgent Christmas target-related things – but knowing that the party starts in an hour and we have to get it done means that we do. And we're always grateful that we did.

DAY 29 PRACTICAL EXERCISE:
THE ANNUAL REVIEW
allow: one hour

Every year, a big highlight for us is delivering our annual review in the office party speech. It's a spirited, upbeat look at the achievements of the previous twelve months.

We'd like to encourage you to give yourself an annual assessment, preferably one with lots of positives. Our own company culture is a good-natured competitive one, so for us the occasion sees a collective fever pitch of excitement at achieving our goals. But even if you don't have employees (yet), there is much to be gained in quietly patting yourself on the back for what you have done well.

Begin with income earned and financial targets met. Count your successes and benchmark them against the previous year.

Secondly, review the tasks you set yourself twelve months ago and put a big tick against those you have achieved. Note down any unexpected challenges that happened along the way.

Finally, focus on any positive feedback you've received over the year, whether that was praise from a colleague, a satisfied client, good customer comments, press reviews or even awards you've been nominated for or won. With this encouraging annual review in front of you, make a list of what you hope to achieve next year.

We hope that this book has helped you overcome many of the initial fears and challenges that you were worrying about before you started reading. You should by now have identified your personal and professional blockers that were preventing you from moving forward on to the next level – and dealt with them. This should have helped you re-envision your goals, together with a path to reach them by. And we hope that you have found support, whether from colleagues, friends, family, resources or a combination of all four, giving you the power to lift the weight off your shoulder.

You've worked hard. And this is the point at which we want to remind you to be kind to yourself. Because whether you are running a business or a department, in order to move *your* company or career further forward it's only you that can do it. You are the only one who understands what it truly takes, so you must praise yourself as much as we ask you to critique.

DAY 30 PRACTICAL EXERCISE:
THE THIRTY-DAY REVIEW
allow: two hours

We'd like you to review what you've done since the first exercise and think about where you've got to. Wherever it is, we want you to be happy with it. Write down the achievements you are proudest of since you began this book – the things you got done and dusted that you had previously thought you would never get around to. The challenges you met or the difficulties you overcame successfully. Keep this somewhere you can look at it now and again, whenever you need a little boost that you have achieved things that once you thought were too hard if not impossible.

If you haven't quite managed to do everything completely or to turn around things that still need to be dealt with – that's okay too. You've got time and the important thing is that you know now what your to-do list contains. That's a whole lot better than the blank feeling of needing to do *something* but not knowing quite what.

Pull up a new document or a fresh sheet of paper and note down all the areas that you need to follow-up on as soon as possible and those that you need to be mindful of periodically, whether that's weekly, monthly or quarterly. Pin this up where you will see it daily. Put reminders in your diary. And as you complete things, tick them off – right where you can see it so you are frequently reminded that you are making progress.

We know that however much you've done since you began the book, the job's not over yet. If you're a builder, you'll keep on building. What you have to watch out for is that the joy of achievement doesn't get buried under the rubble, all the hard stuff that it takes to get that construction under way. You have to keep clearing the rubble away.

Hard stuff can be hard decisions, hard conversations or hard thinking. It is all too easy to leave things be, but we have learned that the only way to set yourself and your business free is to tackle these things as quickly and as honestly as you can. That's why it's important to be organised about documenting what needs to be done, if only to get it out of your hair.

It is made doubly tough to face those things if you are the boss. We have talked to many successful CEOs, past and present, in all industries – it is, and always will be, lonely at the top. No one else is going to look up and try to protect you or make those hard decisions for you. It is your job to care about the business and do what you think is right. Treat your role as the parent to the child (though you must take care not to treat any of your colleagues or employees as children!). Seeing your role at work as a parental one to the business takes the edge off the feeling that you are going it alone. It starts to feel different.

You have the entrepreneur's mindset, remember. That means you will always be clear about how the time and even money invested always makes perfect sense, for so many good reasons.

PARTNER MILESTONES

It's not just us that grew the business on to another level – we're proud to say that many of our partners have too. At the end of 2013, thirty-two partners went up to what we call Enterprise level (over £50,000 in sales over the past twelve months) and seven went over £250,000 for the year. That's on top of the six partners who've passed the million-pound mark.

You will do everything you can, however difficult, to protect, nurture and grow something very special – your business.

We hope this book has given you confidence, certainty and the skills to achieve your goals. You will have fixed those areas that were holding you back – perhaps now you are better at managing people, or have dared to dream bigger than you thought possible before. And if you do get thrown a curve ball now and then, as life tends to do, you know how to deal with it. You know, at the very least, that no matter how successful and driven you are, everyone gets worried or has their bounce knocked back. But you have every right to feel proud of yourself and what you've done. You were prescribed a tough medicine but you've completed the course – well done.

Go ahead, choose a life less ordinary. You deserve it.

Sophie   Holly

Sophie and Holly receive their MBEs in 2013.

WE ASKED OUR PARTNERS

What's your best advice for anyone wanting to grow their business?

Becky Broome: Don't be afraid to be ambitious, whatever that means for you. Whether that is creating a business that is successful enough to support yourself or building a brand that is recognised nationally or even globally. Don't limit yourself, think big and don't be afraid. You are more likely to regret something you didn't do than something you did. We are constantly thinking of ways to progress our business. Even if you are doing well there is always room for improvement, another level you can reach. Be adaptable: if you want to grow your business you have to constantly change and enhance the way you do things.

Highland Angel: I think the most important thing is to stick at it and not to become disheartened. It takes time to build a business and you have to be totally committed if you are going to succeed. If it were easy, everyone would be doing it. A friend of mine gave me the following advice, which I've remembered on various occasions along the way: 'For the first year, you'll support the business, in the second year it will support itself and in the third year it will support you.' This helped me to focus on the bigger picture and keep going during difficult times.

Ellie Ellie: One of our favourite sayings in the office is 'Dreams don't work unless you do' and I think this advice is spot on. Work hard. There may be more talented people out there but there is no excuse for anyone to work harder than you. Make mistakes – I know that sounds like an odd thing to say but make as many mistakes as possible during the first few years of running a business because the more mistakes you make in life and in business, the more you will learn. Don't be afraid of failure, as it's better than having regrets of what might have been. One of the most valuable skills to have while your business is growing is to know your own and your staff's strengths and weaknesses. Never try and do everything yourself, absorb expertise wherever you can from people with experience and invest in professional skills as soon as you can afford to.

Sophia Victoria Joy: Stretch your goals and your vision first. Set out a clear plan and be very ambitious. I have been told time and time again that my goals and visions are too ambitious and maybe I should start smaller or focus on now, but I am totally and utterly convinced that they are in fact achievable. It's the best feeling in the world to prove that they are just that.

The back
pages

These pages are referred to earlier in the book –
they are here to provide extra detail needed for HR admin,
interviews and the financial dashboard.

GET YOUR HR HOUSE IN
ORDER IN A DAY

Conducting your own HR audit will help you identify any problems or gaps that need addressing.

Take a look at this schedule and decide what you want to focus on, having read the chapter People Need People. You will be able to tackle more if it is quiet and you have someone helping. It's essential to commit to finishing these tasks – they will be invaluable to you. Consider doing this at the weekend when you can work in confidence and without interruption. Remember that you have legal obligations to keep any personal data on your employees confidential, so if someone is helping ensure they understand this and can be trusted.

We recommend that you get an independent HR or legal professional to check any employment documentation and make sure it is legally compliant; they can also guide you on any issues that come up as a result of your audit.

Task: Are your employee
records up to date?

Send out an email to all staff asking them to provide you with their most up-to-date details. Include:

* Name and home address.
* Contact numbers and details: mobile, home telephone, email address.
* Bank account details.
* A copy of their passport or another acceptable document to prove your staff have the legal right to work in the UK.
* Next-of-kin details and who to contact in an emergency.
* Details of any business interests outside of work that may cause a conflict of interest.
* Details of any medical conditions or disabilities the company should be aware of.
* Expression-of-wishes forms for those in any pension or life insurance scheme.
* Driving licence and current insurance if your staff drive on company business.

Resources needed: List of staff from payroll; expression-of-wishes forms (what happens to death-in-service benefits and pensions in case of death).

Remember: Set a deadline for this task as you will almost certainly need to chase to get the information you need.

Task: Are your payroll and benefits correct and up to date?

Permanent staff

✳ Are your payroll records up to date?

✳ Check that full-time and part-time staff are on the same benefits (it is illegal to offer less favourable terms to part-time staff).

✳ Do you have all your staff on the right tax codes?

✳ If someone has a loan, do you have an end date recorded?

✳ Book to attend a forum on auto-enrolment for pensions and ensure you know when you need to do this by.

✳ Double-check everyone that is being paid still works for you or is off sick or on maternity leave, and that those off sick are being managed in accordance with your sickness absence policy.

✳ Check that your best, most valuable employees are the ones that you pay well.

✳ Check notice periods have been updated when you have promoted people – for key staff three months is common, for directors six months, for other staff one month.

✳ If you work from home and employ cleaners and gardeners, ensure that the right person pays them (i.e. you personally or the business). Keep very clear records.

Resources needed: List of staff and payroll records.

Temporary members of staff and/or contractors

✳ Are you aware of the twelve-week rule? (After this period, temporary workers are entitled to equal rights with permanent workers, including paid holidays.)

✳ Check they haven't done four years' unbroken service, at which point temporary staff automatically become permanent, thus gaining more employment rights on which you must then follow correct procedures.

✳ If self-employed but solely working for you, check they are not technically in fact an employee.

Resources needed: List of all your temporary members of staff, from agencies, or directly to you; list of any contractors or self-employed staff and the hours they have worked.

Task: Are your staff files complete?

For each staff member you should have the following on hard copy or digital file:

✳ Contract of employment (if more than two months' service).

✳ Offer email or letter.

✳ Copy of references (if you took them).

✳ Copy of passport and/or work permit to show the right to work in this country.

✳ CV or application form.

✳ Interview notes.

✳ Copies of qualifications.

✳ Any other information – requests for flexible working/medical/ disciplinary or grievances, etc.

✳ Job descriptions.

✳ Any correspondence (emails or letters) changing terms and conditions (i.e. pay rises, hours, etc).

✳ Check employment contracts are legally compliant and up to date.

✳ Check that key staff contracts have restrictive covenants (non-poaching and non-compete clauses should they leave) that are specific and enforceable.

✳ Archive, do not destroy, any files of staff that have left.

Resources needed: List of your staff from your accountant or payroll provider to cross-reference with your records; file for each staff member with dividers or an electronic storage system – scan and digitally file each document.

NB: You might get someone to sort this through for you to save time depending on how many staff you have.

Task: Are your recruitment practices and paperwork in order?

✳ Consider your best recruitment channels: agencies/directly via the internet/via LinkedIn?

✳ Negotiate or renegotiate terms with providers. Consider working with one retained provider to get better rates.

✳ Establish the tools for direct recruitment: get your company on LinkedIn. Start with your own profile or add a page to your website.

✳ CVs and interview notes relating to unsuccessful candidates should be kept on file for a year and then archived. File them by surname, by agency or by the month of the interview.

Task: Are you health and safety compliant?

You can't ignore this whatever business you are in.

* Check that you know what your legal responsibilities are to your employees. As company owner you are automatically designated health and safety officer and have a clear duty of care.
* Contact HSE (Health and Safety Executive) for a starter pack – cost £35.
* Do an audit and draft an action plan. Ask your staff questions, such as what they would do if there was an accident.
* Check you have an accident book. It's a legal requirement. Check through it as part of your audit. As well as recording accidents for legal reasons, you should also note 'near misses' to guide you on accident prevention. Act on these.
* Make a list of PPE (personal protective equipment) and who has it.
* Is your building safe? Have you got a handrail? Falling downstairs carrying something is a common accident at work.

Task: Do you successfully train and develop your staff?

* What are your key business objectives and do your staff have the right skills?
* Conduct an annual appraisal – rate your staff, set objectives for them, give them honest feedback and ask for it in return.
* The key thing is to have the conversation and to keep a record of it.

✳ Ensure you cover how they have done and what you expect them to do for the following year. Don't avoid the negatives as they are golden opportunities for improvement on both sides.

✳ Are your staff trained on equipment that requires regular training and certification?

✳ Do your staff lift things? Ensure they get manual handling training.

✳ Do your staff ever work alone in the building? Make sure you exercise your duty of care by establishing a checking-in system.

Resources needed: An appraisal form – design your own, download from the internet or get someone to design it for you, such as an independent HR or career consultant.

Task: Do you have a staff succession plan?

Who are your stars? Do they know? How are you managing their careers?

✳ Conduct stay interviews with key staff.

✳ Review their terms and conditions – can they be offered stock or equity in the business to incentivise or reward continued service?

✳ What would they value to help them stay?

Task: Is your insurance adequate and up to date?

Ensure you have the correct insurance policies and cover:

✳ Employers' liability.

✳ Public liability.

✳ Home insurance: if you work from home your current policy may not
   be valid.

✳ Car insurance if you or staff drive on company business.

✳ Know what additional cover (as part of your insurance cover) you have
   in case you need it.

Resources needed: Copies of all insurance documents relating to your
home and business.

GUIDE TO INTERVIEW QUESTIONS

**This is a template for you to choose from when preparing to
interview a candidate. Use these questions as a basis for your
interviews, but make sure you know before you start what a good
response would be to ascertain whether the candidate has what it
takes.**

✳ Why did this job appeal to you? What is it about this role and this
   business that made you apply?

✳ Why do you believe you would be good at this role?

✳ How would you describe your current (or previous) role?

✳ What have you most liked about your previous recent roles? What have
   you not liked?

✳ Give me an example of something you've done that demonstrates your
   eye for detail/ability to communicate effectively/team spirit/problem-
   solving/adapting to a changed brief.

✳ Have you ever had to deal with an unhappy customer? How did you
   deal with them? Were you able to resolve the situation?

* What achievement in your previous role or personal life are you most proud of? (Someone once said learning to walk and talk – and he wasn't disabled just cocky – he didn't get the job ...)

* At one time or another we have all missed a deadline. Describe the last time you missed a deadline. What caused you to miss it? What did you do?

* Have you ever found yourself in a situation with conflicting priorities that both required a lot of time or effort? How did you deal with it?

* We have all had things go wrong at work. Can you share something that has gone wrong for you and what you now do differently as a result?

* What issue would you consider resigning over and why?

* Why did you leave your last job? (It's important that you are clear about reasons for leaving any recent roles or time gaps in a CV.)

* What would your colleagues say about you? Good and not so good? Is it true?

* If you go home at the end of the day and say to your partner that you have had a wonderful or a terrible day – what has happened to make you feel like that?

* How could you add value to this business and the role?

* What are your salary expectations?

* If we were offering you training or development, what would you want to focus on? (This can be telling if they say they want training on the very area you need them to be already expert.)

* Where do you live? How easy is it for you to get here?

* What's your availability? Do you have any holiday booked over the next few weeks or months?

FINANCIAL DASHBOARD

Financial dashboards are a development of the KPI summary we talked about in Money Talks and are something every entrepreneur should refer to. They will vary depending on the type of business but when looking at the overall health of a business these are some of the more likely measurements and indicators you would expect to see:

Marketing and customer funnel
* Lead sources
* Referrals
* Cost per lead/order
* Repeat customers and frequency
* Active customers as % of total

Sales funnel
* New leads
* Total leads and age
* Converted leads and % of total
* Bookings/orders/sales
* Average order value

Production
* Number of units produced
* Cost and time to produce
* Quality/error rate

Fulfilment and delivery
* Number of days to deliver

* Cost to deliver
* Stock levels
* Return rates

Financial
* Revenues
* Costs to manufacture
* Gross margin
* Expenses
* Profits
* Profit margin
* Cash balance

Customer service
* Number of support calls
* Resolved cases
* Average waiting time and resolution time

Information technology
* Network downtime/Site uptime

Web businesses
* Number of visitors
* Click-through rate
* Conversion rate
* Average time on site
* Basket abandonment rate

Jargon buster

'First, learn the meaning of what you say, and then speak.'

EPICTETUS

A plain-speaking guide to technical terms and the
occasional obfuscating word found either here
in this book or in the world of business.

ABC1 adults: One of several socio-demographic classifications used by
marketers to segment and target their audiences. ABC1 is the most frequently
targeted group, due to their high disposable income. Others are also referenced
but sometimes considered a less lucrative audience in business.

Affiliate marketing: When another website displays a link or banner
advertising your own website. You can pay for this service (through a pay-
per-click scheme, or in commission on resulting sales) or come to a mutually
beneficial agreement with third-party sites (maybe you carry a link to their
website in return).

Audience: Another word for potential customers, and in marketing, the people
or segment to whom your marketing message is aimed. For example, the online
users of a site you feature on or visitors at a sponsored event.

Audit: A systematic examination or investigation into something – could be
finance, data or performance – for a stated purpose.

Balance sheet: A statement of the business's assets (machinery, cash, stock
and so on) and its liabilities (what you owe to suppliers, HMRC and others) at
that point in time.

Banner: A web or display banner is an online advertisement space sold under
an affiliate marketing agreement, through a direct deal with the advertiser,
or via an advertising network. Usually short and wide or tall and thin in
appearance, banners promote traffic to your website from third-party sites
through a clickable design.

Blog: A website publishing experiences, opinions and/or observations – akin
to an online journal – and an increasingly popular channel for business as well
as personal use. Blogs are usually owned and contributed to by one person,

or in some cases a small group, with readers able to interact and comment on 'posts' – whether text, images or both – left by the author.

Bottom-up pricing: A means of calculating the best price point for your product(s), based first and foremost on any production costs. You will also need to look at sales-based and top-down pricing.

Business angel or angel investor: A wealthy individual who uses their own money to invest in a business in return for equity.

Call to action: A term to describe the direction given to consumers by a piece of advertising or marketing material; for example, 'Click here to redeem your voucher' or 'Visit www.notonthehighstreet.com for more information'.

Capital: In the business context, capital refers to any finance or asset owned by a person or company and available for a specific purpose, such as setting up, or investing in, a company.

Capital costs: The amount of money spent on equipment or machinery (otherwise known as capital assets) needed for your business. In accounting, you might hear capital costs referred to as 'fixed assets'.

Capital depreciation: A calculation of the amount by which any capital assets lose value over time, an important consideration when drawing up your P&L forecast.

Cash flow forecast: A spreadsheet showing your business income (money coming in) and expenses (money paid out) over a certain amount of time (usually a minimum of twenty-four months). The cash flow forecast is an integral part of your business plan.

CCFO: Chief commercial and finance officer.

CEO: Chief executive officer.

CFO: Chief financial officer.

CMO: Chief marketing officer.

Consultation period: Any company seeking to make redundancies must have a meaningful consultation period with its employees first. There are rules and regulations that govern this according to the scale of redundancies planned – see www.gov.uk/staff-redundant/redundancy-consultations.

Content management system (CMS): A web-based tool for publishing and editing website or blog content such as text, images, data and video.

COO: Chief operations officer.

Copyright: An exclusive legal right that arises automatically upon creation of a literary, artistic or creative work, protecting that work from copy (and, to certain extents, use) by anyone other than the person who wrote, made or designed it.

Core offering: The primary benefit offered to consumers by your product or service.

Corporation tax: Tax paid to HMRC on the profits of a limited company, at 21 per cent at the time of writing (though lower rates apply for small businesses with taxable profits below a certain threshold). Visit the HMRC website for more information.

Creditor: Any person or business to whom you owe money.

Customer relationship management (CRM): This is a catch-all phrase for systems in a company that have been implemented in order to manage the business's relationship with existing or prospective customers. It commonly refers to the software that allows a company to target customers with tailored emails.

Direct mail: Any piece of marketing material sent directly to consumers, for example an addressed catalogue or a promotional letter to existing customers.

Display advertising: A means of online marketing whereby advertisements to third-party websites appear online in display banners.

Disposable income: The amount of spending or saving money available to a consumer or household once their taxes have been deducted from their income.

Distance Selling Regulations (DSRs): UK legislation designed to protect consumers not physically present at the time they make a purchase from a business. The legislation therefore applies to all transactions made over the phone, online, by email or by mail order.

Distribution list: A group of email contacts, meaning you can quickly and easily send a piece of mail to multiple addresses at once. Distribution lists are commonly offered by email programs and providers such as Microsoft Outlook and Google Mail, and are useful if you need to send a targeted message to contacts that fall within a particular category without inserting each address individually (for example, a press release to all national news desks).

Dividends: An amount paid out to shareholders of a company from after-tax profits.

Domain name: See URL.

Door drop: Any piece of unaddressed marketing material delivered to consumers, for example a company brochure or takeaway menu.

Due diligence: A detailed review of company information that usually takes place before an agreement or sale. The bigger the agreement, the more comprehensive the investigation; venture capitalists, for example, will require an in-depth audit of financial accounts and company history, as well as a personal background check, before signing on the dotted line.

EBITDA: The acronym for 'earnings before interest, taxes, depreciation and amortisation'. In other words, it's the current operational profitability of a business before any of the deductions are made.

E-commerce: The buying or selling of products by electronic means – most commonly online, but email and fax transactions count too.

Economies of scale: The amount of money a business can save when expanding its operations. For example, the cost per unit tends to drop when buying mass-produced items in large quantities, and lower rates of interest are often available to big companies able to borrow large amounts of money.

Elevator pitch: A phrase coined to describe the few sentences that capture your business. It's the pitch a business owner would make if they found themselves sharing a lift with the perfect investor and had just a few seconds to get their message across.

Email marketing: A marketing channel in which specific consumers are targeted by email.

Embargo: A PR term requesting that the recipient of a piece of material does not publish it until a specified date. If you are launching a product or service, or want to release some important information on a certain date, sending the information in an advance press release with an 'embargoed until' date allows journalists to prepare their story in time to coincide with your announcement, with an understanding that your message must not be leaked before that date. A press embargo is not legally binding, but journalists honour such requests so as to maintain good relationships with sources of news-worthy information.

Employee relations: How a company engages and manages its relationships with employees.

Equity: The ownership interest of investors in a company, i.e. the stake in that company they are entitled to in return for their money.

Equity finance: Selling shares in a company as a means of raising money.

Exit: When an investor sells their stake in a company, taking any profits or losses in their shares.

Final written warning: This is the second-highest sanction before dismissal and will stay on an employee's file for a fixed time period. It's used for repeat offenders who have gone through the warning system or for one-off but serious issues. The letter will point out that any subsequent related offences are likely, once investigated, to result in dismissal.

Financial forecast: A calculated prediction of a company's finances over a certain period of time. Drawing up a cash flow forecast and P&L forecast are essential when starting a business, and should be repeated frequently after that.

Fixed costs: Costs necessary in providing a product or service that are not dependent on how many are sold. For example, the cost of renting a premises or monthly internet fees.

Gross: The entire sum of what you get paid, before any taxes (for example VAT) are paid out.

Gross margin: This is the profit made on a product after deducting the direct costs of producing it from the price for which it was sold.

Hidden costs: Costs that you might not initially think of the first time around. When buying a computer, for example, is there any software that you will need to upgrade down the line? Is your sewing machine going to need a regular service to maintain its use? Are you still using the home printer, when you ought to buy a new one?

High-res/low-res image: Image resolution describes the detail a digital image holds, so the higher the resolution, the more detail the image has and the better the quality. High-res is what you need for printing a full-page image on a website, but you only need low-res if you are emailing a picture as a reference (not for printing).

Hosting service: A company that effectively sells space on the web, allowing you to use their hosting servers to hold your website.

Hyperlink: A clickable image or piece of text that directs the user somewhere else, either to another page within the same site or to another website. For example, the text, images and URLs that appear in search engine results that· take you to the chosen page.

Intellectual Property (IP): This is a catch-all phrase that includes the non-physical elements of your business that need legal protection. Intellectual property law is made up of many elements of intellectual property rights (IPRs) including: trademarks, copyright, registered design and unregistered design rights.

Investors: Bodies or individuals (such as business angels and venture capitalists) who put money into a business in return for a share of ownership, or equity.

Key performance indicators (KPIs): The term used to describe factors used in measuring the most important indicators of company performance over an amount of time. KPIs will range from business to business (and department to department), but common examples might include the number of new customers acquired, the percentage of customer service enquiries resolved positively or simply the amount of turnover generated by a particular activity.

Keywords: A marketing term used to describe one or more words commonly used by consumers when searching for a particular product or service. Defining and measuring these words is particularly important for SEO purposes.

Lead: A potential customer.

Limited company: A company owned entirely by its shareholders, with limited financial liability. There are two types of limited company: public and private. Business Link and Companies House can help you find out what the right type of business is for you.

Natural or organic search results: When you type a word or phrase into a search engine, these are the results that appear on the list purely because of their relevance to your enquiry, as opposed to paid search results.

NDA: Nondisclosure agreement – a legally binding contract signed by all parties agreeing to confidentiality, between either private individuals or whole companies.

Net profit: The money left over after all costs and taxes are paid. This can be a negative number, in which case it is a net loss.

Open rate: A term to describe the percentage of recipients who open a piece of email marketing material, as opposed to those who delete without reading.

Overheads: Ongoing costs necessary to running a business, for example rent and utilities, insurance or accountancy fees.

Paid search results: Exactly what it says. Unlike natural or organic results, these appear in premium spots on the search engine results page (usually at the top, or to one side) as a result of PPC advertising.

Patent: A form of intellectual property that protects new inventions, their function and the way that they work to achieve it. Filing for a patent can be complex and expensive, and an invention needs to fulfil certain criteria before it can be protected. The Intellectual Property Office can tell you more.

PAYE (Pay As You Earn): The system used by HMRC to collect income tax and National Insurance contributions (NICs) from employees (which includes directors of limited companies). The tax and NICs are calculated throughout the year, based on the employee's earnings and paid to HMRC. Payroll software is available to ensure this is done; RTI (Real Time Information) is the process that employers must use to submit PAYE information to HMRC on or before each time each employee is paid.

Pay-per-click (PPC): A marketing technique used to promote search results, encouraging traffic to sponsored sites. Each time a user clicks on a paid result, the owner of the promoted website is charged a predefined amount.

PR: Or public relations, as it is now less commonly known. PR falls under the umbrella of marketing, and essentially functions to maintain the public image of a company or person.

Press advertising: Advertisement space sold in newspapers and magazines, in a range of sizes. You can often buy print and online space together within the same publication.

Price point: Quite simply the price of a product or service. You will initially need to determine how much you will sell for by using the bottom-up, top-down or sales-based pricing methods.

Primary research: A means of gathering information directly from consumers, either by observation or by interview. For example, by conducting a survey on your local high street or sending an email questionnaire. Primary research can be time-consuming and you might find that many people say they are too busy to take part but it can be a good way of getting in-depth answers that are directly relevant to your business.

Profit margin: Refers to the money you make after your costs have been paid.

You can increase your profit margin by reducing costs, increasing the price of the product/service sold or by increasing sales while maintaining fixed costs. You reduce your profit margin by increasing costs or discounting your product/service price. But there may be short-term profit losses for long-term profit gains.

Projection: See financial forecast.

Qualitative research: This refers to research into behaviour and what governs that behaviour – the why and how of decision making, for example. Small survey groups, for this reason, often provide just as useful information as large ones.

Quantitative research: Systematic research gathered from a substantial representative sample of respondents, often using mathematical models. Data will be collected using statistics or percentages. It's much more about the when, where and what of, say, decision making.

Reach: A term used to denote the extent or application of a message to customers.

Referral: To recommend a person or a service to another.

Retargeting (also called remarketing): A means of directing a display banner advertisement to targeted customers, normally to incentivise those who have viewed a product online but decided not to purchase.

Return rates: The profit on an investment over a period of time, usually expressed as a proportion of the original investment. The time period is typically a year, so this may be referred to as 'annual returns'.

Return on investment (ROI) and cumulative ROI: Usually shown as a percentage or occasionally a multiple, the revenue or sales return you make on – usually marketing – expenditure.

Revenue: Any money that comes into the business as a result of normal business activities, meaning revenue is usually derived from selling goods or services. Also known as turnover.

Risk capital: A sum of money invested in a business that is at risk of not being repaid. This is most often the case with loans granted by friends and family.

Route to market: How, where and when you sell your product or service.

Run rate (finance): How a company's future performance might look if based on recent achievements. For example, the number of sales predicted for the coming year based solely on those made over the last quarter.

Sales funnel: This is used in many different scenarios but in essence it refers to the reductions in sales prospects as you progress through your sales process. For example, you start with 100 leads for sales; reduced to 50 when half the emails are bounced back from the wrong address; down to 40 at the 'not interested' stage; then to 20 that you are able to schedule one-to-one meetings with and finally you make a sale to three of them.

Sales volumes: The quantity of products or services sold over an amount of time.

Scaling up: As your business revenue grows, you will inevitably need to expand proportionally. This could mean renting larger premises, taking on employees, upgrading tools and equipment, working longer hours and so on.

Search engine optimisation (SEO): A means of marketing your business with the specific aim of it appearing high in the results lists of an online search engine.

Secondary research: Often called 'desk research', secondary research is undertaken by collating and summarising ready-made data – i.e. information collected by someone else and recorded in books, online publications, archives, national statistics and so on. If you know exactly what you are looking for, secondary research can be a lot more productive than primary research, though it's unlikely you will find information tailor-made to your business.

Secured loan: A loan provided by a bank or other lender that is secured against an asset belonging to you or your business. The most common example is a mortgage against property; should you default on repayments, your creditor may take that property and retrieve the value they are owed.

Shareholder/stakeholder: Any person or organisation that owns at least one share, or equity, in a company.

Shareholding/stakeholding: The percentage or proportion of equity owned by a person or organisation relative to the total number of shares within a company.

Social media: The most engaging marketing tool of our time, social media channels such as Twitter, Facebook, Google+ and Pinterest are changing the way businesses promote their products and services, and interact with their customers.

Sole trader: The simplest way to run a business, setting up as a sole trader does not require registering a company with Companies House. You must, however, register as self-employed with HMRC. Keeping records and accounts is straightforward, and you get to keep all the profits. However, sole traders are personally liable for any debts that their business runs up, making this a risky option for businesses that require a lot of investment capital. Business Link and Companies House can help you find out what the right type of business is for you.

Subscriber list: A database of the email and/or postal addresses of people who receive information about your company. It's important to comply with the Data Protection Act when holding such data – visit the Information Commissioner's Office (ICO) website to learn more.

Target demographic: A group of people to whom a company targets its product or service, and logically its marketing and advertising efforts too. Demographics include age, gender, income, health, education, nationality and so on.

Tax deductible: A term describing any costs that can be used to reduce your taxable income and end-of-year tax bill, in most cases because the expense was necessary to the function of your business. The Business Link and HMRC websites can tell you more.

Thumbnails: **Reduced-size images that usually accompany a larger image.** Thumbnails allow the consumer to view multiple images at once – for example of various aspects or colours of a product – and often, when clicked, enable the consumer to view a bigger, high-res version of the selected picture through hyperlink.

Top-down pricing: **To be used in conjunction with bottom-up and sales-based** pricing methods, top-down pricing is a means of ascertaining a suitable price point against what consumers would be willing to pay.

Total transaction value (TTV): **This is a term that we use to make our KPIs** better understood, more relevant and more compelling. TTV is the total amount paid by a customer that comes through the checkout – be that in a single order, a day, a month, a year – including, for instance, delivery costs and VAT. It shows the full extent of transactional activity, even those parts that are not due to come our way, such as VAT.

Trademark: **Your brand's distinguishing mark, represented by a graphically** designed sign or badge. Customers are thus able to identify you and your products quickly. A trademark can be: a logo or symbol (the Nike swoosh); a company name (ACME Ltd); a brand name (Virgin); a sign or shape (the bottle owned by Coca-Cola); a colour (Pantone 151 owned by Orange Brand Services Ltd); or a word, phrase or slogan.

Traffic: **The number of people that use a website, measured in terms of visitors** and page views. The number of visitors to a site will invariably be lower than the number of page views, since only one site visit will be counted regardless of the number of pages that visitor clicks through to. Traffic can be an important KPI and is useful in monitoring how a customer uses your website and for how long. See Google Analytics and Alexa for more information.

Transactional site: **A website on which users can either buy products or book** services.

Tribunal: **Refers to an institution with the authority to judge, adjudicate and** determine employment claims and disputes. In the context of HR, it's referred to as an employment tribunal in the UK. It's not as formal as a court of law although it is often chaired by a judge who sits with two specialist lay members. These represent the employer side (usually with a business background) and the employee side (usually with a trade union background).

Turnover: The total value of sales over a certain period excluding VAT. Also known as revenue.

Unsecured loan: Money borrowed from a bank or other lender which, unlike a secured loan, does not give the creditor any rights over the borrower's assets. This increased risk means interest on unsecured loans is usually higher than on secured loans.

URL: A uniform resource locator (also called domain name or web address), otherwise known as the global address of a website – for example www.notonthehighstreet.com.

USP: The unique selling proposition of your product or service that makes it stand out from its competitors.

Value added tax (VAT): A percentage of the sales price (currently 20 per cent) that a registered business charges a customer and then passes on to the government. A VAT-registered business can reduce this payment by the amount of VAT it is charged by its VAT-registered suppliers. Only businesses with a turnover of more than a certain amount need to be registered for VAT. For more on this, see the HMRC website.

Variable costs: Any expense associated with producing your product or service that changes according to the quantity you sell (unlike fixed costs). For example, raw materials, delivery costs or labour.

VAT threshold: The amount of turnover a company can achieve before needing to register for VAT with HMRC, currently at £81,000. This figure changes annually and businesses have to take the responsibility of checking it.

Venture capital: Money invested in a business by a professional investment company in return for equity in that business.

The directory

'There is nothing like looking, if you
want to find something.'

J.R.R. TOLKIEN

Use this as your quick reference
point for helpful resources.

BUSINESS ADVICE, SUPPORT AND RESEARCH

British Library Business & IP Centre
bl.uk/bipc
The Federation of Small
Businesses
fsb.org.uk
Office for National Statistics
ons.gov.uk
SmallBusiness Advice UK
smallbusiness.co.uk
Tamebay
tamebay.com

COMMUNITY AND SUPPORT

Business Plus Baby
businessplusbaby.com
Enterprise Nation
enterprisenation.com
everywoman
everywoman.com
Mum's The Boss
mumstheboss.co.uk

Makers' Guild
makersguild.org
Meetup
meetup.com

CUSTOMER FEEDBACK SYSTEMS

Feefo
feefo.com
Trustpilot
trustpilot.com

FINANCE

ASC Finance for Business
asc.co.uk
Experian UK
experian.co.uk
FreeAgent
freeagent.co.uk
HM Revenue & Customs (HMRC)
hmrc.gov.uk
Sage
sage.co.uk

HR

Acas – free mediation advice
  acas.org.uk
PeoplePerHour
  peopleperhour.com
Directgov – official UK government
advice on payroll, employment rights
  gov.uk/browse/employing-people
Directgov – official UK government
advice on pensions
  gov.uk/workplace-pensions
Health and Safety Executive – advice,
information pack and helpline
  hse.gov.uk
Simply-Docs – standard
employment documents and
contracts
  simply-docs.co.uk
Trainer Bubble – staff training packs
  trainerbubble.com

LEGAL ADVICE

Anti Copying in Design
  acid.eu.com
Chartered Society of Designers
  csd.org.uk
Copyright Licensing Agency
  cla.co.uk
Design and Artists Copyright
Society
  dacs.org.uk
European Trademarks and Designs
Registry
  oami.europa.eu
Institute of Trademark Attorneys
  itma.org.uk
Intellectual Property Office
  ipo.gov.uk
The Law Society
  lawsociety.org.uk
Own-it – intellectual property
advice
  own-it.org

MARKETING

Affiliate marketing
Affiliate Window
  affiliatewindow.com
Commission Junction
  uk.cj.com
Rakuten LinkShare
  linkshare.com
Tradedoubler
  tradedoubler.com
Webgains
  webgains.com

Display advertising

Criteo
  criteo.com

Google Adsense
  google.co.uk/adsense

Google Display Network
  google.co.uk/adwords/
  displaynetwork

Struq
  struq.com

Email marketing

Campaign Monitor
  campaignmonitor.com

MailChimp
  mailchimp.com

SmartFocus
  smartfocus.com

Performance tracking

Alexa
  alexa.com

Google Analytics
  google.com/analytics

Picture editing

Adobe Photoshop
  photoshop.com

GIMP
  gimp.org

Picasa
  picasa.google.co.uk

Mister Clipping
  misterclipping.com/uk

Search engines and SEO

Bing
  bing.com

Google
  google.co.uk

Google Adwords
  adwords.google.co.uk

Yahoo!
  uk.yahoo.com

Social networking, blogging and videos

AddThis
  addthis.com

Bitly – link shortener
  bitly.com

Facebook
  facebook.com

Google Blogspot
  googleblog.blogspot.com

Instagram
  instagram.com

LinkedIn
linkedin.com
LikeMinds
wearelikeminds.com
Pinterest
pinterest.com
TED
ted.com
Tumblr
tumblr.com
TweetStats
tweetstats.com
Twitter
twitter.com
Wordpress
wordpress.com
Wordpress (advanced)
wordpress.org
YouTube
youtube.com
Vine
vine.co

PROFESSIONAL PROFILING

Belbin – Belbin Team Roles
belbin.com
The Myers & Briggs Foundation –
Myers-Briggs Type Indicator
myersbriggs.org

Pearson TalentLens
talentlens. co.uk

REGISTRATIONS AND REGULATIONS

Companies House
companieshouse.gov.uk
Companies House WebCheck service
wck2.companieshouse.gov.uk
Data Protection Act – Information
Commisioner's Office (ICO) guide
ico.gov.uk/for_organisations/
data_protection.aspx
Directgov – official UK government
direct.gov.uk
Distance Selling Regulations –
Office of Fair Trading guide
oft.gov.uk/ds-explained

SURVEY TOOLS

RationalSurvey
rationalsurvey.com
Smart-Survey
smart-survey.co.uk
SurveyMonkey
surveymonkey.com

ACKNOWLEDGEMENTS

Just as with the shaping of notonthehighstreet.com, many people have helped us to get this book into shape, and we owe them all personal and heartfelt thanks.

Writing a second book with Jessica Fellowes has been – if that were ever possible – an even more enjoyable and positive experience than the first, so our thanks to her and to her family, Simon, Beatrix, Louis and George, for their support in its many different forms.

Our agent Caroline Michel together with Rachel Mills at Peters Fraser and Dunlop, and the editorial team at Simon & Schuster including Carly Cook, Mike Jones and Jo Whitford, all played a huge part in planning, shaping and finessing the manuscript, as did Humphrey Price. Others at Simon & Schuster, including Dawn Burnett, Ally Glynn, Elinor Fewster, James Horobin, Dominic Brendon, Rik Ubhi and Jon Stefani, have all brought great commitment to the book's publication and marketing, and much appreciation goes to Kate Wright and Lydia Ripper who brought their fresh and engaging design to its pages.

Contributing to the content have been some of the most inspiring people we've had the good fortune to work with over the years. Many thanks to Ruth Cornish, independent HR consultant; Kevin Greenleaves, business coach; Anton Teasdale, facilitator; and Verity Lewis, business coach. We have drawn wisdom from stylist Amanda Erritt, as well as Jane Cunningham and Philippa Roberts of Pretty Little Head.

From the team at notonthehighstreet.com came much expertise for which we would not dream of taking credit – it is instead due to Andy Botha, Ben

Carter, Claire Durney, Nic Forster, Jenny Hyde, Antony Lea, Kate Lynas, Lizi Riehl, Rebecca Vanstone, Victoria Swift, Julie Turner, Sarah Wilson. Any mistakes, however, are most definitely ours.

Our thanks to our board for their continued support: Mark Esiri, Ben Holmes, Davor Hebel, Laurel Bowden, Victor Hwang. And to the many friends, staff and colleagues of the business, old and new, who are too many to name but have so enthusiastically and often generously given their time and wisdom to help us thrive.

Our small business partners have always been the very backbone of notonthehighstreet.com, and while we try to share all we know with them, it is really we who are learning from them, every day. So we cannot thank them enough for being at the heart of our story; special thanks to those who contributed content so honestly to these pages. Equally, we have learned much, and owe even more, to our customers, who have played such an essential part in shaping notonthehighstreet.com.

And finally, and most importantly, we are ever in the debt of our friends and our families who have been so patient and kind through the making of the business, and of this book: our parents Penny Vincenzi, and Sally and Robert Tucker; our sisters Polly Harding, Emily Gunnis, Claudia Vincenzi and Carrie Gateshill; and last but unquestionably not least, Sophie's husband Simon and their children Ollie and Honor, and Holly's partner Frank and their son Harry. We feel privileged that the business has brought us such wonderful opportunities but you brought so many more and make it all very much better.

INDEX